BERLITZ®

RHODES

 Library of Congress Catalog Card No. 75-13202.

Printed in Switzerland by Weber S.A., Bienne.

17th Printing
1993/1994 Edition

How to use our guide

- All the practical information, hints and tips that you will need before and during the trip start on page 97.
- For general background, see the sections The Island and the People, p. 6, and A Brief History, p. 11.
- All the sights to see are listed between pages 21 and 66, with suggestions on daytrips from Rhodes from page 67 to 69. Our own choice of sights most highly recommended is pinpointed by the Berlitz traveller symbol.
- Entertainment, nightlife and all other leisure activities are described between pages 70 and 80 and from page 90 to 96, while information on restaurants and cuisine is to be found on pages 81 to 89.
- Finally, there is an index at the back of the book, pp. 126–128.

Although we make every effort to ensure the accuracy of all the information in this book, changes occur incessantly. We cannot therefore take responsibility for facts, prices, addresses and circumstances in general that are constantly subject to alteration. Our guides are updated on a regular basis as we reprint, and we are always grateful to readers who let us know of any errors, changes or serious omissions they come across.

Text: Steve Leonard and Bob Fresh
Photography: Geraldine Kenway and Christopher Mascott
We are particularly grateful to Michael Lambrou and Vicky Nicolopoulou for their help in the preparation of this book. We also wish to thank the Greek National Tourist Organization for its valuable assistance.
Cartography: Falk-Verlag, Hamburg.

Contents

Maps

Cover picture: Mandráki Harbour. *Photo pp. 2–3:* Palace of the Grand Masters

The Island and the People

The wonders of Rhodes... warm, ever-present sun—and everything that's happened under it for the past 5,000 years. This eastern Mediterranean island has a history and culture so varied and intriguing that many visitors end up spending more time seeing the sights than lazing on a beach.

The past is all around you on Rhodes. It's beneath you —ancient Greek remains often come to light when a cellar is dug up—and above you—the stadium overlooking Rhodes Town was used by athletes training for the Olympics, centuries before the birth of Christ.

Rhodes is the gods' own place in the sun: according to Greek mythology, the sun god Helios chose it as his bride and blessed it with light, warmth and lush vegetation. A similar myth recounts that Helios fell in love with the nymph Rhodon and named the island after her. The word *ródon* probably meant "rose"—a flower that grows in profusion here,

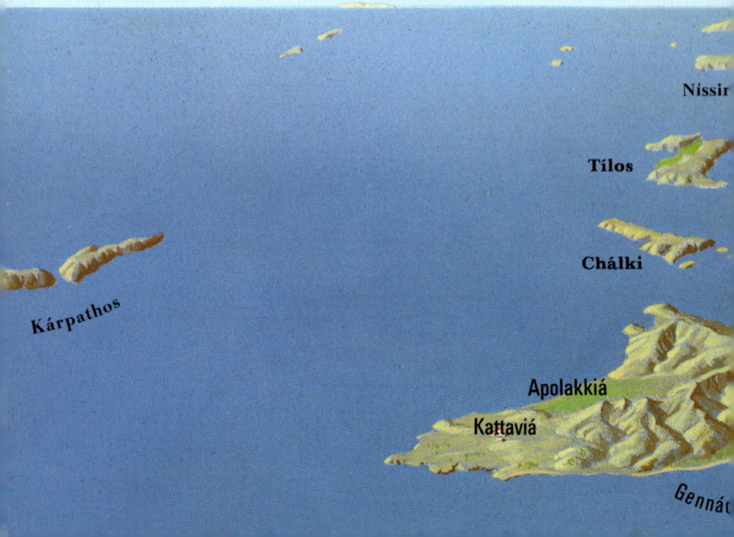

as do hibiscus, bougainvillea, jasmine and honeysuckle.

In the morning, when you open your blinds on this flower-scented island, the chances are about 300 out of 365 that you'll be greeted by sunshine and blue skies. In fact, from April to October, the odds are almost 100 per cent in favour of sunny skies with temperatures in the 80s or above.

In the 1950s, the Greek government showered the island with a new ray of light—tourism. Foundations and swimming pools were dug, and hotels, *tavérnas* and discotheques soon sprouted. Within 20 years, the annual tourist figure reached almost half a million. Many came from Scandinavia. Another 65,000 visitors called in on the island on cruise ships for a day or two, anchoring in one of the magnificent harbours.

Only 12 miles off the coast of Turkey, Rhodes is a natural stopping-off point for Egypt, the Holy Land or southern Europe. In fact, much of its turbulent history, as well as its wealth, is directly attributable to its location in an island chain right in the path of eastern Mediterranean navigational routes.

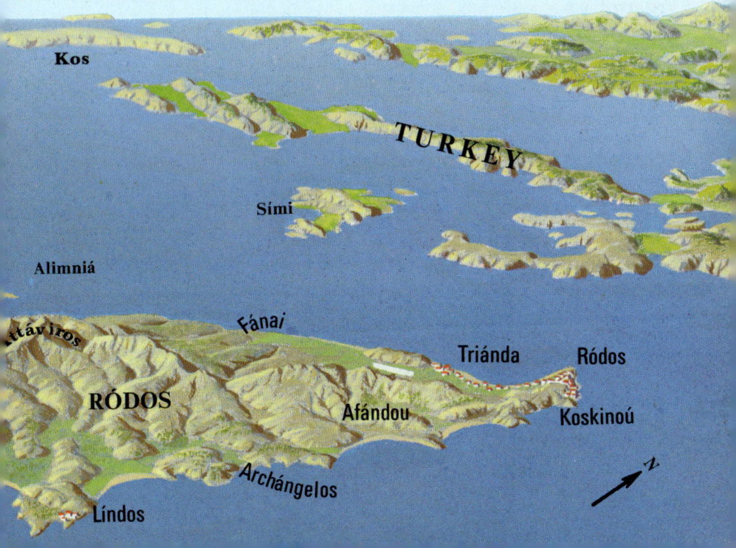

The chain, called the Dodecanese, consists of over 200 islands of all sizes and shapes, but only 18 of them are presently inhabited. Thirteen* of the islands have local governments and comprise what is officially referred to as the Dodecanese in geography books. Their administrative capital is Rhodes.

The population of the 540-square-mile island is 72,000. At the time of the Trojan War in the 12th century B.C., however, it was five times as great, for Rhodes was then one of the world's principal centres of wealth and culture as well as a military power in its own right.

Towering above the scene today, floodlit at night, are the walls, parapets and fortifications of the Knights of the Order of St. John. The crusader knights established their hospital in Rhodes in the 15th century, after being forced out of the Holy Land. They managed to hold off the Moslem tide for two centuries, until finally Suleiman the Magnificent captured the island in 1522.

Beneath the impressive walls, in some places up to 40 feet thick, Rhodes is a bustling city. Its modern shops, boutiques and smart restaurants add a dash of 20th-century chic to an old town of busy, narrow and evocative streets. Lively *tavérnas* and animated cafés—drowned in the aroma of Turkish coffee and the blare of *bouzoúki* music—lend a splash of colour to shady medieval squares and overlook busy harbours filled with pleasure boats.

At Kámiros, on the island's west coast, lie the remains of an ancient abandoned city. At Líndos on the east coast, a temple to Athena looms high on a cliff above a perfectly sheltered cove where the apostle Paul is said to have landed in A.D. 51 on his way to Syria.

There are beaches and coves to explore everywhere along Rhodes' 138 miles of coastline. And, for the alpinist: there's a 3,975-foot-high mountain to climb.

But this island, bursting as it is with history, sun and duty-free shops, offers still another attraction that is far from being negligible. It's an

* In Greek, Dodecanese means literally "12 islands". The baker's dozen includes Astypaléa, Chálki, Kálimnos, Kárpathos, Kássos, Kastellórizo, Kos, Léros, Níssiros, Pátmos, Ródos, Sími and Tílos.

integral, dynamic and delightful part of Greece.

When among Greeks, you will sense their pride, dignity and self-respect (that they themselves call *filótimo*). Perhaps it reflects an awareness of the glorious achievements of Greek civilization. In any case, it certainly accounts for a head held high through centuries of foreign domination.

Their greatest pleasure comes from such things as the family, their surroundings, music and dancing.

Boutiques flourish along the arched, medieval streets of Rhodes Town.

In a manner befitting life on the island of the sun god, Rhodians spend most of their time outdoors. Markets, *tavérnas,* cafés and even cinemas are in the open. Open, too, are the doors of people's homes, for there's virtually no theft, nor is there a jail. Honest, direct and friendly, Rhodians love life and enjoy people. They convey this to you in many ways.

In Greek, *xénos* means "stranger". But true to Greek character, *xénos* also means "guest".

The whole family is enmeshed in the business of repairing the nets.

A Brief History

Rhodes' strategic position on vital trade routes in the eastern Mediterranean fundamentally influenced the course of its history—and a tumultuous history it has had, too. For nearly 5,000 years, conquerors and empire builders have attacked, sacked and exploited the island.

It is a long tale of foreign domination right up to the first half of the 20th century, when the Italians occupied the island. But today's foreign invasion—in the form of over half a million tourists annually—is a welcome one to the Rhodians, for it has brought prosperity and stability to a land once continually ravaged.

The island's earliest history, dating back to the Stone Age, is sketchy and clouded by myths. Certain indications prove that the first inhabitants, a primitive, rugged people from Asia Minor, could make fire and hand-work soft metals and that they fashioned simple tools and made pottery. From about 2500–1500 B.C., during the Bronze Age, they were overrun by waves of invaders–Carians from Anatolia, Phoenicians from present-day Lebanon and highly civilized Minoans from Crete. The latter colonized Rhodes and built shrines for moon worship at ancient Ialyssos (now called Filérimos), Lindos and Kamiros.

1,000 Ships Against Troy

But the most significant early invaders were the Achaeans from the Peloponnese, the Greeks of Homer's *Iliad,* who had pushed south through Athens. By 1500 B.C., these amphibious warriors had attacked and occupied both Crete and Rhodes. When the Achaeans launched their famous 1,000 ships against Troy, Rhodian ships (nine, according to Homer) sailed with Agamemnon's fleet. The ten-year war ended in the destruction of Troy (present-day Hissarlik in north-western Turkey), but also exhausted both the resources and the spirit of the conquerors. They were no match for the tall, blond, savage Dorians who swept through Greece about 1100 B.C.

Although the Dorian occupation ushered in a dark age of despotism which lasted for centuries, their fusion with the Aegean people eventually produced the classical period of Greek civilization. As for Rhodes, it was encouraged to develop independently and by 700 B.C., under Dorian charter, it set up the Hexapolis, a six-city trading league. One of the Rhodian cities, Líndos, minted its own coins (money had, in fact, just been invented in Asia Minor) and sent merchants off to colonize the Costa Brava in Spain, Gela in Sicily and Nea Polis, known today as Naples.

A 2nd-century B.C. warship carved in the rock below Líndos acropolis.

In the 5th century B.C., a large Persian force dispatched by Darius reached the Aegean; only Greece stood in the way of its westward drive. Rhodes joined forces with the Persians and suffered defeat with them at Marathon (490 B.C.). When the Greeks sank King Xerxes' fleet at Salamis 10 years later, 40 Rhodian ships were among the victims. The Athenian league was founded soon afterwards, and Rhodes became a taxpaying member.

Rhodes Rides the Crest

Growing in importance as a maritime power and centre of trade and finance, Rhodes tried to remain neutral, except when its trading interests were at stake. Thus, she supported successively the Athenian league and then Persia against Macedonia. But when it was clear that Alexander the Great was worthy of his name, Rhodes sided with him, benefitting substantially from trading concessions with Egypt, Macedonia's next conquest. After Alexander's death in 323 B.C., Rhodes refused to join an expedition by one of his successors against Ptolemy I,

The Colossus of Rhodes

The shattered *helepolis* Demetrius left behind was sold to finance a statue of Helios, the sun god, protector of Rhodes. The location of this statue, known as the Colossus, remains shrouded in mystery.

The traditional belief that the Colossus straddled the entrance to Mandráki harbour, permitting ships to pass between its legs, and that it held above its head a torch that shone far over the sea has been discounted. Its construction would have required a foundation on solid land. More recent theories place it near the Palace of the Grand Masters.

The Colossus was over 100 feet tall—or about 30 feet shorter than New York's Statue of Liberty. Sculptor Chares of Lindos, took 12 years to cast the Colossus in bronze, finishing the work about 290 B.C. A masterpiece of technical* and artistic achievement, it was considered one of the Seven Wonders of the ancient world.

But both the work and its creator were ill-fated. The sculptor killed himself in despair when he discovered an error in his calculations (which an assistant had to correct), and the Colossus cracked at the knees and crashed to the earth in about 225 B.C., during one of Rhodes' periodic earthquakes. It had stood as a triumphant memorial to Rhodian military prowess and artistic craftsmanship for less than 70 years.

The oracle at Delphi warned the population not to restore the statue, and it remained where it had fallen for over 800 years. In the mid-7th century A.D., the Arabs, led by Moabiah, sacked Rhodes and sold off the bronze as scrap to a Jewish merchant from Syria. The 20 tons of bronze were probably carried away by some 90 camels. But true to the colossal nature of the legend, it is said that 900 camels were required.

the Macedonian general who had become the king of Egypt. This led to an onslaught by Demetrius the Besieger, in 305 B.C., which Rhodes survived—an impressive feat. The battle itself has become legendary.

Demetrius had mobilized an army of 40,000 troops, supported by a vast fleet and an ingenious siege machine known as the *helepolis,* a bronze-plated oaken tower on wheels (10 storeys high) with built-in archers' nests, grappling hooks and deadly catapults. Pulled right up to the ramparts of the fortified city, by hundreds of slaves, the juggernaut hurled stone missiles while massive battering rams pounded the walls. Six thousand Rhodian defenders,

The Divine Family

The pantheon of Greek gods and goddesses and their Roman equivalents often engenders divine confusion in the ordinary mortal. Below are the names of a few heavenly beings important to Rhodes:

Greek	*Roman equivalent*	*Attributes*
Aphrodite	Venus	goddess of love, daughter of Zeus
Apollo	Apollo	god of light, the arts, reason, poetry, son of Zeus
Artemis	Diana	goddess of hunting and sometimes of childbirth, daughter of Zeus
Athena	Minerva	protector of cities, daughter of Zeus
Helios	no direct Roman equivalent, though later identified with Apollo	god of the sun, protector of Rhodes
Poseidon	Neptune	god of the sea, brother of Zeus
Zeus	Jupiter	King of Olympus, god of heaven and earth

held out for nearly a year, repulsing every attack with determination and inventiveness (they even deployed fire boats in the harbour) until Demetrius finally withdrew.

The story of the *helepolis* attack against Rhodes is vividly told in Lawrence Durrell's *Reflections on a Marine Venus*.

In 166 B.C., to punish Rhodes for failing to side with her against Perseus of Macedonia, Rome took away Delos

Famed Rhodian statues at Archaeological Museum—upper left: *Helios, Rhodes' protector;* lower left: *Aphrodite, goddess of love;* right: *Zeus.*

(a Rhodian protectorate), declaring it a free port attached to Athens. Rhodes was thus deprived of substantial tax income from port duties. Two years later, Rhodes concluded an alliance with Rome. Thereafter, the island was rewarded or punished according to the level of its military support for Rome's constant wars.

Rhodes Attacked and Sacked

The alliance brought Rhodes a new dilemma—which side should it take in Rome's internal struggles and civil wars. Rhodes supported Pompey against Julius Caesar. But Caesar, after defeating the Rhodians, was forgiving and re-cemented the alliance. Then the assassins of Caesar, Cassius and Brutus, demanded Rhodian help in their war against the senate. When this was refused, Cassius besieged, conquered and sacked the city, plundered 3,000 statues, and left "nothing but the sun".* Almost all of this precious art was destroyed when Rome burned in July of A.D. 64.

By the 2nd century B.C., despite its problems with Rome, Rhodes had won renown as a centre of cultural and intellectual activity within the Roman empire. Visitors to the school of rhetoric, probably based on the acropolis just outside the town of Rhodes, included Cicero, Julius Caesar, Pompey, Brutus, Cato the Younger, Cassius and Mark Anthony.

Christianity took root in Rhodes during the 1st century A.D. aided by St. Paul, who visited the island on his way to Syria, some 20 years after the Crucifixion. But Rhodes was not to find peace or stability.

The island was a target for succeeding waves of invaders. It was plundered by the Goths in A.D. 263, overrun by both Persians and Arabs in the 7th century, and then unceasingly harassed by pirates and corsairs. Although nominally part of the Byzantine empire, Rhodes was completely on its own as far as defence was concerned.

By the 11th century, followers of Mohammed had conquered Jerusalem, implanted their faith in Persia and North Africa, converted the Turks

* A reference to a famous sculpture of Helios' chariot by Lysippus, which was too heavy to remove.

and occupied half of Spain. To Christians the threat to their faith and to the security of Europe was ominous.

Rhodes' ties with western Europe were strengthened—first through resumption of trade with Venice, then, in 1097, with the appearance of the Crusaders on their way to the Holy Land. In 1191, England's King Richard the Lion-Heart and King Philip Augustus of France landed in Rhodes to recruit mercenaries. Byzantium was captured by the Crusaders 13 years later. Then the tide of battle turned, and by 1291, the Christian army was forced off the beaches at Acre, today part of Israel.

Among the retreating soldiers were the Knights of the Order of St. John, founded in Jerusalem more than two centuries earlier. They had run a hospital near the Church of the Holy Sepulchre for pilgrims who succumbed to the hardships of travel. But during the Crusades, the knights became more and more militaristic. Forced to fight off repeated Moslem attacks they learned the value of fortified walls, even in the Holy Land.

The Knights Buy an Island

When the order was forced to regroup, they settled first on Cyprus. But, as the Moslem threat to that island grew, they decided Rhodes would make a better bastion.

Since the stubborn and fierce Genoese pirates who had taken over Rhodes in 1248 would not let them settle there, the knights decided to buy the island. An authentic bill of sale was drawn up and wit-

15th-century Knights' Hospital now houses the Archaeological Museum.

nessed. But they still had to fight for their newly acquired property, defeating—and subsequently massacring—the Turkish mercenary garrison assigned to the island by the Byzantine emperor. By 1309, the knights had started the elaborate fortification of Rhodes. They settled in, maintained their hospital, continued to improve the defences and fought off Moslem assaults for the next 213 years.

The knights were housed in inns, according to their native language. Eight different "tongues" were represented—those of France, Germany, Italy, Spain,* Auvergne, Provence and England. Each group had a defence perimeter to secure against attack.

They fortified the outlying islands as well, and their walls and castles are still to be seen on Kálimnos, Léros, Chálki, Tilos, Kos, Níssiros and Sími. On both land and sea they were formidable warriors, undaunted in their defence of the Cross. In 1444—numbering no more than 600, plus 5,000 Rhodian supporters—they resisted attack by the sultan of Egypt. Thirty-six years later they brilliantly outfought the forces of Mohammed II (the Conqueror).

Suleiman Attacks

In 1522, Sultan Suleiman I, the Magnificent, moved against Rhodes. Infuriated that the knights tolerated marauding pirates from Spain and Malta, yet intercepted Turkish pilgrim ships enroute to Mecca, he decided to get rid of the Christian bastion once and for all. His massive force landed near Iályssos on June 24. Two hundred ships, shuttling back and forth from the mainland, landed soldiers, military equipment, food and supplies—including Hungarian horses, Mesopotamian oxen, Syrian camels and Thracian mules. A month later 150,000 troops laid siege to Rhodes with the sultan in command.

The knights found themselves isolated. Much of Europe lamented the plight of the last of the Crusaders... but ignored their distress calls.

In four and a half months, Suleiman lost 50,000 men trying to penetrate the fortified city. The Turks were on the verge of giving up when a trai-

* Later split into Castile and Aragon, thus including Portugal.

tor revealed that the Christians were at the end of their tether. Suleiman decided to go all out and finally breached the walls. The Rhodian population, facing famine, called for a truce.

And so, on January 1, 1523—after 145 days of siege—the 180 surviving knights were allowed to depart honourably for Malta, where they became known as the Knights of Malta. They took with them several thousand Rhodian Christians, their church banners, art treasures and sacramental relics. And for nearly four centuries, until 1912, Rhodes remained a minor Turkish possession.

Four hundred years of occupation should have left an indelible imprint on the Rhodians. But Ottoman rule, both on Rhodes and elsewhere in the Mediterranean, was sleepy and decadent. The Greeks and Turks each went their own way, with little assimilation of one culture by the other.

The Turks built—and destroyed—little. Occasionally a church was converted into a mosque. The Grand Master's Palace became a cattle barn. The once-noble inns were turned into barracks. The Turk, said French writer Charles Cottu, "was content to squat on his carpet, puffing on his pipe throughout the centuries".

But Rhodes, linked closely to Greece and its culture through the Orthodox church, still remained very firmly Greek.

In 1821, mainland Greece revolted against the Turks and eventually won independence. Rhodes, too, tried to throw off its yoke but failed, suffering brutally as the Turks quashed the revolt. Not until the years before and after World War I was the Ottoman empire at last dismembered, leaving in its stead the Balkans, the Dodecanese and Aegean islands, the Arab world and North Africa. Italy scored the first victory against the Turks and, through the Treaty of Lausanne in 1912, took over the Dodecanese Islands—ostensibly in trust for eventual union with Greece.

Unlike the Turks during their period of domination, the Italians immediately set to work excavating and restoring classical sites and constructing roads, homes and public buildings. Although the Rhodians suffered hardship under the occupation, the Italians did make Rhodes a more accessible island and started its tourist development.

A Retreat for Mussolini

However, it became increasingly clear that Italy had no intention of returning the Dodecanese chain to Greece.

Governor's Palace blends Arabic, Gothic and Venetian architecture.

In the late 1930s, both the Greek language and the Orthodox church were outlawed on Rhodes, and plans were made to turn the island into a summer retreat for Italy's rulers. The Dodecanese Islands were to crown the Italian claim of *mare nostrum* in the Mediterranean.

After the Mussolini government fell in 1943, German troops landed on Rhodes and took over all Italian defence positions and military bases. The islands were finally liberated by British forces in 1945 and, after a period of United Nations trusteeship, were united with Greece in 1947.

Greece made immediate plans to develop tourism on the island. Duty-free concessions were granted, hotels were built, and tourist facilities expanded.

So, now, once again, Rhodes is being invaded. But this time—and perhaps for the first time in its 5,000-year history—simply by people in search of sun and a taste of the island's remarkable past. And each year the tourists are flocking to Greece's most popular resort in ever-increasing numbers.

Rhodes Town

Pop. 32,000

Rhodes *(Ródos)* is really two towns—the old and the new. Most tourists, however, make a beeline for the Old Town which is certainly the most memorable. We've divided this part of the town into sections: the knights' quarter, or Collachium, and the Turkish quarter. As you'll pass the Jewish quarter on your walking tour of the Turkish area, we've included it within the section about mosques and minarets.

Soaking up the sun; traditional handicrafts produced in the age-old way.

Knights' Quarter

This quarter can be visited on foot in a few hours, and if you only have a short time to spend on Rhodes you should head there first. For, in wandering through the narrow streets and squares, you'll get a feeling of the island and its history. You'll be swept back to the fascinating days of the 14th–16th centuries when the Knights of St. John made Rhodes their stronghold.

There are intriguing little passageways and courtyards off the narrow streets to be explored. Be on the lookout, too, for special vantage points providing spectacular views of the harbour and of the Aegean Sea below.

The moat between the inner and outer walls of the Old Town never contained water: it simply discouraged invaders from putting up siege towers. Under the knights, Rhodes' fortifications evolved as weapons changed from arrow and spear to cannon and gunpowder. Over two centuries, the Crusaders constantly strengthened the walls, making them more massive and curving them to deflect cannonballs.

Finding Your Way

To facilitate your finding your way, this guide refers to all street locations in their transcribed Greek form—the one you'll see on street signs throughout the island. To simplify things, however, we've dropped certain titles like *vasiléos* (king), *vasilíssis* (queen) and *ethnárchou* (archbishop) sometimes listed on street signs. We've also omitted writing the word *odós* (street) each time in the text, but have used *platía* (square) which often appears on signs and local maps.

Certain local guide books and maps translate principal streets into their English or other language equivalents. We've often used the English equivalent in the first reference to the street and thereafter have employed only the Greek transcribed version.

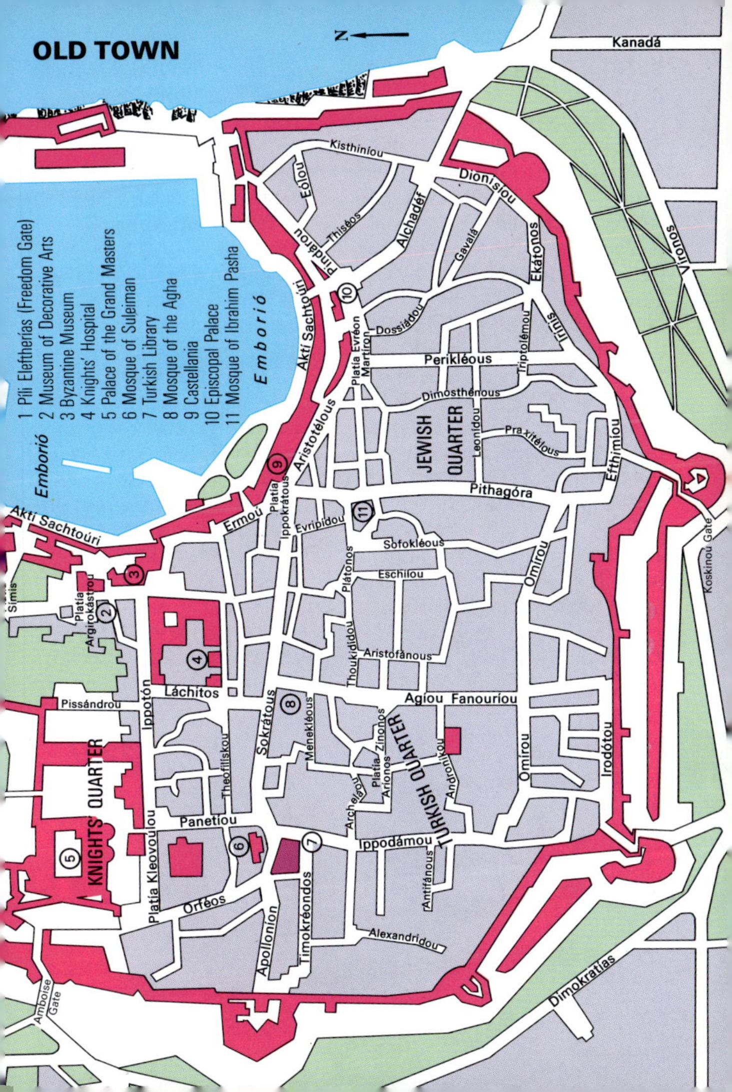
OLD TOWN
N
1 Píli Eleftherías (Freedom Gate)
2 Museum of Decorative Arts
3 Byzantine Museum
4 Knights' Hospital
5 Palace of the Grand Masters
6 Mosque of Suleiman
7 Turkish Library
8 Mosque of the Agha
9 Castellania
10 Episcopal Palace
11 Mosque of Ibrahim Pasha
Emborió
Emborió
Aktí Sachtoúri
Aktí Sachtoúri
Kanadá
Kisthiníou
Eólou
Thiséos
Pindárou
Alchadéf
Dionisíou
Gavalá
Ekátonos
Víronos
Dossiádou
Triptolémou
Trínis
Platía Evréon Martíron
Perikléous
Dimosthénous
Aristotélous
JEWISH QUARTER
Leonídou
Praxitélous
Efthimíou
Pithagóra
Platía Ippokrátous
Ermoú
Evripídou
Sofokléous
Plátonos
Eschílou
Omírou
Koskinoú Gate
Símis
Platía Argirokástrou
Thoukidídou
Aristofánous
Láchitos
Ippotón
Pissándrou
Agíou Fanouríou
Sokrátous
Meneklēous
Zínonos
TURKISH QUARTER
Platía Aríonos
Archelaou
Andronikou
Omírou
Irodótou
KNIGHTS' QUARTER
Theofiliskou
Panetíou
Ippodámou
Platía Kleovoúlou
Antifánous
Orféos
Timokréondos
Apollonion
Alexandrídou
Dimokratías
Amboise Gate

They're as thick as 40 feet in some places.

In fact, you'll see real cannonballs, usually stacked in pyramids, throughout the Old Town. Near the Italikí Píli (Italian Gate) schoolboys play football in the moat using these medieval missiles as goalposts. The iron balls were ammunition for the Turkish cannons; the limestone and marble ones were hurled by catapults of a previous epoch.

Start your tour by entering the Old Town through the **Píli Eleftherías** (Freedom Gate) —thus it was named by the Italians who saw themselves as liberators of the island from Turkish oppression. The name took on another significance when the Italians themselves left in World War II.

You're now on **Platía Símis,** where you'll see one of the few ancient vestiges in the Old Town: the ruins of a 3rd-century **Temple of Aphrodite.** Be sure not to miss the magnificent view of Emborió harbour from Sími Gate.

Try to imagine the waterfront scene as it was five centuries ago. Fourteen white-sheeted windmills turn slowly in a gentle breeze. Stevedores employed by the knights are unloading provisions. Tons of saltpetre, to be ground into gunpowder, are hoisted from a caïque. Pine casks of wine from Crete are unloaded from another boat. Carts creak under heavy loads of grain destined for the knights' cellars. And, surveying the scene, are

Temple on Platía Símis, built 2,000 years ago to honour Aphrodite.

two mounted knights in red tunics with white crosses.

Now head up the gentle slope to Platía Argirokástrou. The **fountain** in the centre was discovered by Italian archaeologists in a church near Arnítha. Some purists say it doesn't belong here, though most people find its setting quite pleasing. Behind the fountain stands a 14th-century edifice thought to be the original hospital of the knights. It later supposedly served as an armoury and is now the headquarters of the Greek Archaeological Service.

To your left, as you face the fountain, is the entrance to the **Museum of Decorative Arts.** If you're not pressed for time, this collection of Rhodian folk art is well worth a visit (see page 75). Also facing the square is the **Inn of the Tongue of Auvergne,** built in 1507. The building now houses government offices. The outside stairway, typically Aegean in style, leads to a gallery, and the inn's main entrance has a fine Gothic doorway.

Further along, past a street of arcaded shops, you'll come to the **Panagía tou Kástrou** (the Virgin of the Fort), formerly known as the Mosque of Enderum. Originally built as a church in the 13th century, it has had a variety of "owners". In 1523, having expelled the knights, the Turks converted the church into a mosque by replacing the steeple with a minaret. Many Christians were executed here at that time, which is why it's sometimes called "the red mosque". It is now the Byzantine Museum.

Entering Platía Nosokomíou (Hospital Square), you can catch a view up Odós Ippotón, the Street of the Knights, perhaps the most famous medieval thoroughfare in all Europe. But before proceeding up Ippotón, take a look at the **Knights' Hospital,** one of the most interesting buildings in the Old Town. It was to build this infirmary and care for the sick that the Knights of St. John came to the island and constructed their walls, moats and fortifications.

Built on Roman ruins, the hospital was begun in 1440 and finished about half a century later. It's now the Archaeological Museum of Rhodes (see also page 75).

The arched main entrance leads into a courtyard and the three arches on each side lead

RAYMOND BÉRANGER

1365 1374

ROGER DE PINS

1355 1365

PIERRE DE CORNEILLAN

1354 1355

DIEUDONNÉ DE GOZON

1346 1353

HÉLION DE VILLENEUVE

1319 1346

FOULQUES DE VILLARET

1310 1319

The Knights of St. John

Founded in the 11th century by a wealthy family from Amalfi near Naples, the Knights of St. John on Rhodes never numbered more than 600 and came from the most noble families of Europe. The German knights, for example, had to prove at least three generations of noble lineage.

After taking vows of chastity, obedience and poverty, they lived in seven groups according to nationalities, or "tongues": English, French, German, Italian and Spanish. Provence and Auvergne, independent regions at that time, were also represented. The Spanish tongue later split into the tongues of Aragon and Castile.

Each nationality lived within a compound called an inn under an appointed leader, or prior. The knights walked in pairs and left their walled domain only on horseback. About 5,000 Rhodian Christians were the support personnel of the community and the hospital.

The grand master was elected for life by a majority of nationalities. France, usually supported by Provence and Auvergne and thus outnumbering all other nationalities, was the key tongue—and 14 of the 19 grand masters were French. Of the remaining five, two were Italian and three Spanish. French was the order's spoken language while Latin was used in official documents.

While the defence of sections of the city wall was entrusted to certain tongues, the tongue of Italy commanded the knights' fleet. Outside Rhodes Town, the knights added to their defences by building about 30 fortresses—like those at Líndos and Monólithos—strategically placed around the island and linked by a communications network of bonfires, smoke-signals and homing-pigeons. Additional fortresses were constructed on the outlying islands.

ROBERT DE JUILLY

1374 1377

FERDINAND D'HÉRÉDIA

1377 1396

PHILLIBERT DE NAILLAC

1396 1421

ANTOINE FLUVIAN

1421 1437

JEAN DE LASTIC

1437 1454

JACQUES DE MILLY

1454 1461

RAYMOND ZACOSTA

1461 1467

G. B. DEGL' ORSINI

1467 1476

PIERRE D' AUBUSSON

1476 1505

AIMERIE D' AMBOISE

1505 1512

GUY DE BLANCHEFORT

1512 1513

FABRIZIO DEL CARRETTO

1513 1521

PH. VILLIERS DE L'ISLE ADAM

1521 1522

to store-rooms, some of which are now rented by local merchants. The sick-ward of the knights occupied the floor above. Four rounded columns frame arched Gothic windows, forming a bay that housed a chapel. A bas-relief in the centre depicts two angels bearing the coat-of-arms of the Order of St. John.

On entering the courtyard you'll see stone missiles, piled in pyramids. The larger ones are said to have been used in catapults during the famous siege of Rhodes by Demetrius in 305 B.C. The Rhodian lion, surveying the courtyard from behind a mosaic from Kárpathos, dates from the 1st century A.D.

The hospital could care for approximately a hundred patients. About 30 canopied beds were located in the first-floor sick-ward; small "cells" behind them were probably used for isolating contagious cases.

What kind of patients were tended here? There are many conflicting stories. No doubt the knights needed an infirmary to care for their own sick, and, with plagues sweeping the islands of the eastern Mediterranean, it's possible that the hospital served as an early form of quarantine station. On the other hand, evidence does exist that the beds were reserved for a select roster of nobles. What is certain is that the hospital evolved from its original Christian purpose of ministering to pilgrims outside the walls of Jerusalem.

Museum courtyard—an ideal spot to take a break from sightseeing.

The **Archaeological Museum of Rhodes,** also on the first floor, is one of the island's real treasures (perhaps the word "treasury" is more appropriate, for its collection of ancient coins is outstanding). The museum's statues, Mycenaean vases and jewelry excavated from sites around the island should not be missed; some of the objects date back to the 9th century B.C.

Most intriguing among these artefacts is the famous marble statue of Aphrodite from the 3rd century B.C. Washed ashore one day in 1929, tangled in fishermen's nets, it's known as the **Marine Venus.** If you've read *Reflections on a Marine Venus*, by Lawrence Durrell, you'll know all about the statue. There's a kneeling Aphrodite, too, from the 1st century B.C., unearthed in Rhodes Town in 1912. Often referred to as the *Aphrodite of Rhodes,* this statue of the goddess of love holds her long, wavy hair out to the sun after emerging from the sea.

Don't miss the marble head of **Helios,** the sun god, thought to be from the 2nd century B.C. and discovered near the Inn of Provence, not far from the spot where Helios' temple is believed to have stood.

Other items worth seeing: a small head of Zeus, found on Mount Attáviros; a life-like head of an athlete, in all probability a boxer; and a six-foot-long grave slab from Kámiros. This classic 5th-century B.C. bas-relief depicts Krito bidding farewell to her dead mother, Timarista. Krito's hair is cut short, a traditional sign of mourning.

If you're ready for a rest—or a pause for reflection—the attractive, sunlit garden on the first floor is just the place. (There's a clean lavatory close by, too.)

Leaving the infirmary and the museum, it's time to see how the knights lived; the inns of France, Italy, Spain and England are all grouped in this immediate area.

The **Inn of England,** just across the square from the hospital, has had more than its share of bad luck. Built in 1483, it was destroyed by an earthquake in 1851. After a long period of disuse, it was rebuilt in 1919 when the Italians restored the Old Town. Then during World War II, the inn was severely damaged by shelling. It was the British, appropriately, who restored the inn again in 1947.

Had the Turkish siege taken place a decade later, the English knights would have missed it. For the Tongue of England broke with the Order of St. John a few years after Suleiman's victory in 1522. Their departure from the order followed the pope's excommunication of Henry VIII and the beginning of the Protestant Reformation.

Now stroll up **Ippotón**, a narrow, cobblestoned street. Two archways near the far end seem to bring the medieval façades lining the narrow street even closer together. The mood is austere and sober, and at night it's easy to imagine the scarlet-cloaked knights patrolling the street with dim lanterns casting eerie shadows on the massive stone walls—the silence broken only by the echoing clang of horseshoes on the cobblestones.

You'll come first to the **Inn of Italy.** Over the sculpted doors is emblazoned the em-

A stone relief in Rhodes Archeological Museum.

Fleur-de-lis emblem identifies the impressive Inn of the French Tongue.

blem of Fabrizio del Carretto, a grand master who died a year before Suleiman's assault.

Next door is a small residential **palace;** the façade bears the coats-of-arms of the French grand masters Aimerie d'Amboise and Villiers de l'Isle Adam. Although there is still some question about the purpose of the palace, it is generally believed to have been the residence of Villiers. (Villiers succeeded del Carretto, commanded the knights' defence against the Turks and, ultimately, had to give the order to lower the Christian banners in defeat.)

Opposite the palace is the original main gateway of the Knights' Hospital, leading directly to the sick-ward. Just beyond the hospital, behind a wrought-iron gate, is a charming, shaded **garden** with a Turkish fountain. The museum stores relics here among palm trees and shrubs. The remains of a 15th-century building are probably those of an inn of one of the Spanish tongues, for the door is in the Catalan or Aragonese style. It may have been destroyed by an earthquake or in the gunpowder explosion of 1856 (see page 31). (The site of the Inn of the German Tongue, also destroyed at some point, remains a mystery as well.)

Facing the garden are the **Inn of France,** its chapel and the residence of the chaplain of the Tongue of France. This impressive group of buildings clearly illustrates the predominant rǫle of the French knights in the order (see page 26).

The coats-of-arms on the inn's façade belong to the Order of St. John and to the two grand masters who built it, d'Amboise and d'Aubusson. The date above the pointed arch of the main entrance, 1492, is the year the building was begun—the year Columbus discovered America.

The façade is worthy of more than a passing glance, for it is the most beautiful and richly ornamented one of all. Notice the typically Gothic interplay of lines. For example, in the long, bold horizontals above the arched store-rooms and in the roof pattern against the four vertical, semi-circular turrets. The result is a well-ordered and elegant structure, a difficult achievement considering its long façade on the sloping street.

One of the oldest buildings in the street is the **French Chapel,** with its niche for the Blessed Virgin and Child. You'll notice the arms of many of the grand masters. The escutcheon of one of the first grand masters, Raymond Béranger (1365–73), gives an

The Gunpowder Explosion

The gunpowder explosion of 1856 inflicted more damage to the Old Town than Suleiman the Magnificent's 150,000 troops.

Some time in the 16th century, the Turks hid a stockpile of gunpowder in the Palace of the Grand Masters or the Church of St. John. Afterwards, the cache was forgotten.

Then, one night in 1856, lightning struck a turret of the palace and fire broke out. The flames quickly spread through the passageways and tunnels joining the palace to the church... and suddenly an enormous explosion shook the entire island.

The raging fire spread out of control as far as the harbour. When the smoke finally cleared the toll was enormous. About 800 were dead, the Church of St. John and the Inn of England were levelled, and the Grand Masters' Palace left a burned-out shell. The 14th-century stained glass in the Orthodox Church of St. Mary (now the Byzantine Museum) and various landmarks on Ippotón and Platía Nosokomíou were also destroyed.

Not till the Italians arrived, more than 50 years later, was any attempt made to restore these medieval treasures.

indication of the chapel's age.

Next door is the chaplain's residence, now housing the Italian vice-consulate. A few steps further along are the last two inns of the street—the **Inn of Provence** on your right and the **Inn of Spain** on your left. The buildings, dating from the early 15th century, are less ornate than the imposing Inn of France.

Beyond the second archway to the left stood the Church of St. John, the knights' principal house of worship. The church was blown up in the gunpowder explosion of 1856. A replica (although some critics don't consider it a very authentic one) was built by the Italians in 1925 at Mandráki harbour (see page 44).

At the top of Ippotón you enter Platía Kleovoúlou. Now that you're more familiar with each building, look back down the full length of the street for an overall impression. Ippotón looked just the same when the knights left for Malta in 1523.

Unfortunately, the scene changed soon afterwards. The Turks occupied Rhodes and billeted their troops in the inns. Pressed for space, they built ramshackle wooden balconies from the upper stories, turning the once orderly street into a colourful but cluttered pot-pourri of architecture.

Steps lead to the tranquil inner courtyard of one of the medieval inns.

When the Italians arrived, their archaeological teams set to work immediately, meticulously restoring the street to its 16th-century appearance, removing every trace of the four centuries of Turkish alteration or neglect. The entire Old Town was, in fact, renovated in the same manner. Only mosques or buildings judged to be of cultural value were left alone.

The masterpiece of the Italian archaeologists and architects is the **Palace of the Grand**

The austere and imposing entrance of the Grand Masters' Palace.

Masters on Platía Kleovoúlou. The Turks had turned it into a prison, and after centuries of neglect it was in a shambles. Then, in 1856, even this was destroyed when gunpowder in the palace vaults exploded.

Greek scholars say the Italians should have torn down the remaining ruins and excavated, for they believe there may be an early Greek temple underneath.

The decision to rebuild rather than dig was political and came directly from Mussolini. The palace was to be used as a summer residence for the rulers of Italy. Restoration was completed just before World War II.

By most accounts, the palace contained 158 rooms, a lavish residence, to say the least, for a grand master who took vows of poverty. Now about 15 of the rooms are open to the public. There are magnificent views of Rhodes and the harbour from some of them. This is a panorama you shouldn't miss.

You'll notice some fine Roman and early Christian mosaics in the rooms. These are not part of the original furnishings, but were removed from the nearby island of Kos by the Italians. The most famous is a 1st-century A.D. representation of the nine muses covering the floor of an entire room.

The statues in the courtyard are from the Hellenistic

Twice a week, tourists are permitted to walk around the medieval walls.

period, many of them brought from Kos. At the foot of the grand staircase there's a small chapel containing some Roman and early Christian objects. Before you leave the courtyard, be sure to notice the two inscriptions near the entrance. One is dated 1940, "the 18th year of the Fascist era". The other, carved in Greek, reminds the "unconquered Dodecanese people" that they have succeeded in preserving "under all foreign occupation that inexhaustible fountain of the eternal Greek civilization: the ideal of freedom". It's dated 1947.

As you leave Platía Kleovoúlou turn right into Orféos, a street shaded by plane trees. First you'll see St. Anthony's Gate, which is often used by visitors to enter the Platía Kleovoúlou. A little further along is **Amboise Gate,** built by Grand Master d'Amboise in 1512. Here you'll get a good idea of the extensive fortifications surrounding the Old Town. You approach the gate by a stone bridge. Beyond the gate's massive stone arch, you cross onto a triple-arched bridge over an outer moat. While on this bridge, have a look back at the gate's imposing façade—further strengthened by two squat round towers. Amboise Gate conveniently leads to the new section of Rhodes Town.

If you turn left upon leaving Platía Kleovoúlou, you'll follow what was the south periphery of the medieval inner wall which divided the knights'

This is the gate d'Amboise built.

bastion from the remainder of the Old Town.

Each stretch of the massive outer **medieval wall** between the gates and the towers was called "a curtain" and was defended by a particular nationality.

The English and Spanish knights had a particularly difficult task defending the southern sections, for the land here rises outside the walls, thereby making them more vulnerable to attack. This explains why the fortifications at this point are even more extensive, with towers and a double moat.

Now you can understand why it took Suleiman the Magnificent six months and 150,000 troops to crush this Christian stronghold.

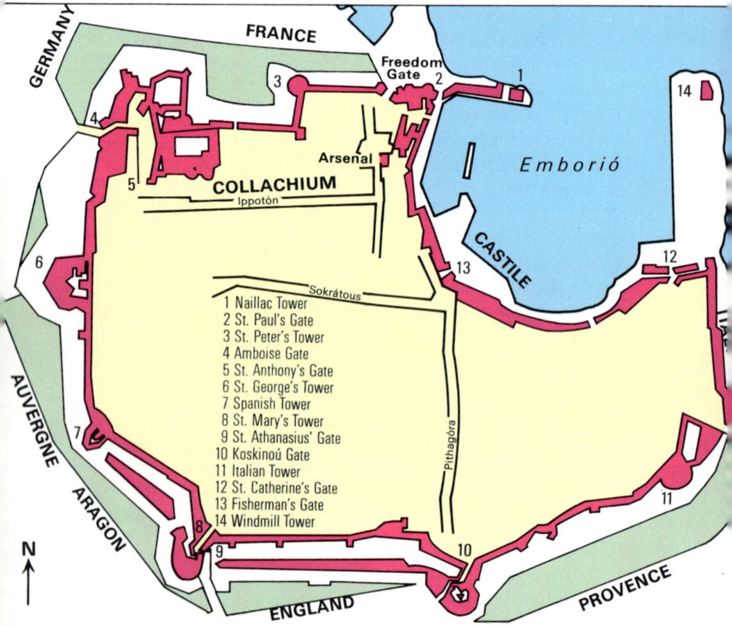

KNIGHTS' DEFENCES

Turkish Quarter

A good place to start your walking tour of Turkish sites is Platía Kleovoúlou. Stroll down Orféos, the shaded street lined with plane trees, until you come to the clock tower on your left. From here down to the harbour stood the inner wall separating the Knights' quarter (Collachium) from the rest of the fortified town. Outside this inner wall, Greeks, resident Europeans and Jews lived in a city within the city. Under Turkish rule, Greeks were obliged to leave the confines of the inner wall by sunset. Violators were beheaded.

There was a 15th-century watch-tower here, later used as a Turkish signal post. An earthquake toppled it in 1851.

Continuing a little further, you'll come to the **Mosque of Suleiman,** the biggest and most important in Rhodes.

Suleiman the Magnificent, the most powerful of the Turkish sultans, brought the Ottoman empire to its zenith under his rule from 1520 to 1566. After conquering Rhodes in 1522, the Turks immediately began to build a mosque in his honour. It was completely reconstructed in 1808; services are still conducted there today.

The portal of the mosque is said to be from a church that once stood on this site. Inside, the mosque is spacious, quiet and pleasing. (Most of the other mosques on the island are in a state of neglect and disrepair, despite the existence of a small Turkish population.)

On leaving the mosque, you'll be at the top of Sokrátous. To the right is the **Turkish library,** stocked with Arabic and Persian manuscripts in glass cases. Especially noteworthy are two exquisitely decorated Korans—one dated 1412 and the other 1540.

Now you can make a choice as to which direction to take. If you prefer to do some souvenir shopping, head down **Sokrátous.** Here you'll be inundated by ceramics, icons, daggers, trays, pots, jewelry and bric-a-brac (see SHOPPING, page 80). Among all the razzle-dazzle, you'll have to look very closely to find the **Mosque of the Agha,** or Turkish commander. It's on your right, about half way down—its wooden, stilt-like legs stumbling out into the street.

But if you're not quite up to shopping at this point, make your way back to Ippodámou—and then take your first left into Archeláou. You'll soon arrive at Platía Aríonos. The **Turkish baths** here were built in 1765. They were destroyed by bombs during World War II and subsequently reconstructed. If too much sightseeing is getting you down, here's your chance to steam away your aches and pains for a while (bring your own soap and towels; closed on Sundays). But in any case, it's worth a look inside to see the vaulted reception room with its worn, white-

Odós Sokrátous: Turks enlarged their houses by adding wooden balconies.

marble floor. There's a small admission fee.

For a less exotic unwinding, you may want to have a drink at the café on Platía Aríonos. Enjoy the atmosphere of this picturesque square, which is surrounded by ancient buildings. The minaret you'll see is part of the **Retjep Pasha Mosque.** It was at one time the most beautiful mosque in Rhodes—built in 1588 of material from several churches. It's now abandoned.

Make your way back to Sokrátous and follow it to the bottom until you reach Platía Ippokrátous. You'll see a Turkish fountain graced by a tiny minaret. On this square are the remains of the medieval courthouse, also known as the Tribune of Commerce or the **Castellania.** The fleur-de-lis and alligator gargoyles are similar to those on the Inn of France. This building was, in fact, completed in 1507, under the French Grand Master d'Amboise, just two years before the inn was finished.

The courthouse once extended to the harbour walls. Its ground floor was used as a kind of merchants' stock exchange; on the floor above, disputes were settled under the legal code of the knights. You can still see the sockets that held banners when the court was in session.

Facing the harbour, turn right on Aristotélous and wander along a short way until you come to Platía Evréon Martíron (Square of the Jewish Martyrs) and the old **Jewish Quarter.** The drum-shaped **fountain** in the centre of the square is faced with beautiful blue tiles decorated with shells and marine creatures. Three large bronze sea horses —heads touching to form a pyramid—cap this unique, unpretentious gem.

The **episcopal palace** on the square, a pot-pourri of Gothic and Renaissance architecture, housed the archbishop of the

Drum-shaped sea-horse fountain in Square of the Jewish Martyrs.

Greek Orthodox Church just prior to Suleiman's invasion.

Evréon Martíron commemorates recent history. In 1934, there were 6,000 Jews living in the centuries-old Jewish quarter. By 1939, about 4,000 had emigrated. When the island was taken over by German troops in July 1943, the remaining 2,000 were assembled in this square and transported to concentration camps in the Third Reich. Only 50 survived. Today seven Jewish families—about 30 people—are left on Rhodes.

At the end of Odós Sokrátous, Suleiman's reconstructed mosque.

The synagogue nearby on Dosiádou is open to visitors.

From Evréon Martíron, walk down the small street just to the left of Aristotélous until you reach Damagítou. Here you'll find the **Mosque of Ibrahim Pasha.** The illegitimate son of a Greek sailor, Ibrahim was sold into slavery and trained as a soldier and servant by the Ottoman Turks. He soon rose to high favour, married the sultan's sister and all but administered Suleiman's empire from 1523 to 1536. And then Ibrahim was strangled on the sultan's orders—without warning or explanation.

The mosque was built in 1531 and later restored by the Italians, who also added the new minaret. Under the plane tree, just next to this mosque, Greeks who violated the curfew decree were beheaded.

From here, you can wander through the streets of the old bazaar, making your way toward Sokrátous for some of the souvenir shopping you may have postponed earlier. Or, heading south you'll have time for reflection as you follow the quiet streets hugging the old walls—from the Koskinoú Gate down towards the harbour.

New Town

Under Turkish rule, the Greeks moved outside the walled city into what came to be called the Néa Chóra, or New Town. This area was first settled in ancient times—and new construction today still unearths remains of old civilizations. The commercial section in the northern part of the city, with its hotels, shops, administrative buildings, banks, cafés and restaurants, is less than 100 years old.

Make the starting point for a stroll around town the office of the Tourist Police. It's at the corner of Makaríou (named in honour of Archbishop Makarios of Cyprus) and Papágou.

Going down Makaríou to Platía Kíprou (Cyprus Square), you'll come to the heart of the shopping district. Passing scores of clothing and jewelry shops, boutiques, souvenir stands and fellow tourists, turn down Gallías towards the port. You imme-

Beyond the bathers, the aquarium marks island's northernmost point.

NEW TOWN
1 Tourist Police
2 Post, Telephone and Telegraph Office
3 Governor's Palace
4 Church of St. John
5 Town Hall
6 New Market-place
7 National Theatre
8 Aquarium
9 Mosque of Murad Reis
10 Nautical Club
11 Fort St. Nicholas
12 Temple of Aphrodite
13 Palace of the Grand Masters
14 Son et Lumière Show
AEGÉON PÉLAGOS
Akrotírio Koúmbournou
Mandráki
N
Platía Vasiléos Pávlou
Platía Vassileos Georgiou
Platía Akadímias
Platía Arch. Chrisánthou
Platía Kíprou
Platía Neórion
Kalímnou-Lérou
Kassou
G. Papanikólaou
N. Mandilára
Dragoumi
Amerikis
Iérou Lóchou
Dilgeráki
Alexándrou
Ammochóstou
Ikostis Pemtis Martiou
Eleftherias
Ethnarchou Makariou
Diákou
Alex. Papágou
El. Venizélou
Papalouká
Dimokratías
Ippotón
Sokrátous
Akti Miaouli
Akti Boúbouli
Gallías
Orféos
Láchitos
Pindou

diately come upon an exotic, Turkish-style heptagonal building which is the **Néa Agorá** (new market-place). The arcaded structure encloses an inner courtyard with stands of fresh fruit, vegetables, meat, fish and other seafood. Any one of the cafés or restaurants in the square is a good spot to stop and take in the sights, sounds and smells of the market scene.

Néa Agorá faces **Mandráki harbour,** which once sheltered the knights' galleys. Now yachts, excursion boats and light cargo craft moor here. The name, meaning sheepfold, reflects the commercial function of the port in earlier days.

Mandráki is guarded by the famous Rhodian landmarks—the **statues of a stag and a doe.** But these aren't the only deer you'll see on Rhodes. There are real ones running wild in the mountains. They were brought to Rhodes at the suggestion of the oracle of Delphi. At one time, the island was overrun by snakes, and the smell of deer was said to repel them. The plan seems to have worked, and Rhodes acquired a symbol as well as a herd.

The three drum-shaped stone **windmills** were built during the Middle Ages to mill grain for departing cargo boats. Their jib-like sails still turn in the breeze but the millstones came to a halt years ago. Another 14 windmills, destroyed in an earthquake, dotted the breakwater of Emborió, the commercial harbour at the foot of the Old Town. Today, Emborió is used for larger ships. A third harbour, Akándia was constructed by the Italians before World War II as an industrial shipyard and dry-dock.

At Mandráki, you can take local pleasure boats for day trips and visits to neighbouring islands. If you feel like roughing it—and can shrug off an occasional spray from the warm sea—try a trip on one of the traditional Aegean caïques, heavy, broad-beamed fishing boats that have been used for centuries in this region.

St. Nicholas Fort, at the end of the pier, was built during the 15th century as an additional defence against Turkish attack. It's now a lighthouse. A chapel inside is dedicated to St. Nicholas, Orthodox patron saint of sailors.

The government buildings along Mandráki were all added during Italian control of the Dodecanese and are constantly criticized by everyone from art historians to the local population. They are massive and austere, but the principal criticism is that they look Italian, not Greek.

The buildings you'll pass are the courthouse, the harbour-master's office and the post office. Across the street, on the harbour side, is the **Church of St. John.** This is a replica of the church that once stood opposite the Palace of the Grand Masters in the Old Town. Now the island's principal church, it's the seat of the archbishop of the Dodecanese.

Just beyond the church you'll come to the Governor's Palace *(Nomarchía)*, reminiscent of the Doges' Palace in Venice. On the side facing the sea is a square, named after Greek Adm. Periklís Ioannídis, who signed the *énosis,* or union agreement, when the Dodecanese islands were united with Greece in 1947.

On the street side of the palace, a square named after King George I of Greece contains the town hall, the National Theatre and around the corner, the Classical Theatre of Rhodes. The building at the northern end of the harbour is the Nautical Club—for members only. Nearby is the Elli Club, a beach club charging nominal admission for

Windmills in Mandráki Harbour once ground grain for departing caïques.

changing facilities. The public beach begins here and stretches all the way around the tip of the island, continuing down the western shore.

Look for an elegant white minaret near the beach club. This marks the **Mosque of Murad Reis** and the **Turkish cemetery.** Murad Reis was the chief buccaneer of the sultan's fleet; he was killed during the final series of attacks against the knights in 1522. His tomb is in the circular structure next to the mosque. Both buildings are entered through a shady, elegantly paved courtyard. Before entering the buildings, remember to remove your shoes in accordance with Moslem practice.

Sheltered under pine and eucalyptus trees, the cemetery is peaceful and, to Western eyes, exotic. Simple, somewhat pointed stones mark women's graves. The men's headstones are crowned by carved turbans.

Burial places for the sultans' more important civil servants are protected from sun and falling leaves by ornate porticos. Some say a shah in exile from the Persian court is entombed here.

Heading north towards Akrotírio Koúmbournou at the tip of the island, you'll come to a solitary building, the Rhodes **aquarium** *(Enidrío)*. Once inside, go down the spiral staircase to a large underground room designed to look like the ocean floor. Here you'll peer at octopus, spotted morays and trigger-fish. It's

The minaret of Murad Reis Mosque (left), *with its cemetery nearby.*

open until 9 p.m. and is an ideal destination for an evening stroll.

Along this northern beach, one day in 1929, the statue known as *Aphrodite of the Sea,* or the *Marine Venus,* dating from the 3rd century B.C., was washed ashore. You can now see it in the Archaeological Museum of Rhodes (see page 28).

Beneath fragrant pines, Turkish dignitaries rest in relative peace.

But the remains of the fabled Colossus of Rhodes, one of the wonders of the ancient world, are nowhere to be seen. Local postcards portray it astride Mandráki harbour, but, according to historians, it probably stood near the Palace of the Grand Masters (see page 13).

Surroundings of Rhodes Town

Either by bus, rented car or cruise boat, you should make your way down the east coast to the ancient village of Líndos. It will be one of the highlights of your trip to Rhodes. Another worthwhile excursion is along the west coast to Kámiros, an ancient city that's believed to have flourished during the 16th and 15th centuries B.C. (see LÍNDOS, page 53, and KÁMIROS, page 62). But closer to home, no more than a quarter of an hour from the centre of Rhodes Town, you'll find some other awe-inspiring sites.

MONTE SMITH

You can get to Monte Smith (Smith's Hill) on the No. 5 bus, leaving from the station near the Néa Agorá. If you decide to walk, make your way to Diagoridón and follow it out of town. It's less than two miles—and the uphill climb is gradual.

Try to save this excursion for the end of the day. For, from the summit of Monte Smith, the view of the Turkish coast, the island of Sími and the straits—with the western sea glittering in the setting sun—is a spellbinder. It's the view that British Admiral Sydney Smith enjoyed for several years while monitoring the movements of the Napoleonic fleet. When the French abandoned Egypt in 1802, Sir Sydney was recalled to London, but his name has remained on the hill that is crowned by the **Temple of Apollo.**

The Doric temple was—and still is—a landmark to ships at sea. Destroyed by the same earthquake that brought down the Colossus in about 225 B.C., it was partially rebuilt by the Italians in the 20th century.

Rhodes' principal acropolis* was located here. (Some archaeologists think the remains of a second acropolis are beneath the Palace of the Grand Masters in the Old Town.)

* It means "hilltop fortress" in Greek.

Doric columns, remains of Rhodes' ancient acropolis on Monte Smith.

The **theatre** below the temple has been restored, so don't be too surprised by the rows of dazzling white marble seats. Only the three bottom rows remain from the 3rd century. Some guides claim that this was the location of the famous School of Rhetoric—and that scholars, not actors, addressed the outdoor audience seated here.

If so, the academics would certainly have been disturbed by the athletes, for the **stadium** nearby dates from the same period. The partially restored stadium is typical of those used for the first Olympic games.

An ancient theatre or classroom of a famous school of rhetoric?

RODINI PARK

If you're looking for some outdoor fun in the evening or a beautifully wooded and tranquil spot during the day, Rodíni Park may be just the answer. Landscaped by the Italians, the park is a paradise of picturesque streams, paths, oleander bushes, flowers, cypress and maples. Rodíni, too, has its claimants as the site of the Rhodes School of Rhetoric.

There's a former necropolis, or cemetery, nearby. One tomb, carved in the rock—and decorated with half-columns in the Doric style—stands out prominently. Known as the **Tomb of the Ptolemies** *(Táfos ton Ptoleméon)*, it dates from the Hellenistic period and was restored by the Italians in 1924.

Ptolemy was the general of Alexander the Great who conquered Egypt. He succeeded the Pharaohs, and his descendants ruled from Alexandria for over 200 years; the last of the lineage was Cleopatra. Historians consider it highly unlikely that any of the Ptolemies were buried on Rhodes. The Rhodians probably mislabelled the monumental tomb because of its similarity to other structures in Rhodes Town named in honour of Ptolemy.

There's a restaurant and night club in the park, but the famous Rodíni Wine Festivals have been discontinued; travel agents, however, are forever concocting new ones in new places (but old style, lots of wine, typical meal, old village, etc.).

To get here by car, take Route 1, which runs along the east coast. The park is just three kilometres from town.

KALLITHEA SPA

Although the Italians tried to promote Kallithéa as a spa for the treatment of rheumatism, gout, diabetes, kidney and liver ailments (the waters are claimed to have been drunk by Hippocrates), they never succeeded, and the buildings have fallen into disrepair. But the small bay is excellent for swimming and skin-diving.

From Rhodes Town, there's a half-hourly bus service to the spa. By car, direction Líndos, follow the signs to Thérme Kallithéas. It's about 10 kilometres from Rhodes Town.

Excursions

East Coast to Líndos

The acropolis at Líndos, perched high above the sea on a rocky plateau, is perhaps Rhodes' most spectacular sight. And yet, when you wander through the village below, you'll find it hard to believe that this was once the most important city on the island—with colonies as far away as Spain—before the city of Rhodes was even founded.

Only 55 kilometres from Rhodes Town, it's ideal for a day's excursion. The journey along the eastern coast takes you through lush scenery on a wide asphalt road, past Rodíni Park (see page 49) and picturesque villages.

A new road—new, that is, in parts—appreciated by those with little time to spare, skirts the coast. However, for more leisurely—and for more rewarding—sightseeing, the villages on (or just off) the former main road have a lot to offer.

The first village you'll come to, about six kilometres from Rhodes, is Asgouroú. The town was once Turkish, and you'll see the minaret of the mosque off to the right.

The homes, courtyards and gardens in the hilltop village of Koskinoú—a few kilometres to the left of Asgouroú—are especially charming and well-kept. It's a pleasant little spot for a stroll. Nearby you'll see a Voice of America transmitter, beamed towards the Middle East.

Eight kilometres beyond Asgouroú, there's a turn-off to the long, sandy beach at Faliráki. Relatively crowded, it's undergoing a hotel boom (see page 91). And a few kilometres beyond, overlooking the Bay of Afándou there's an 18-hole golf course (see page 94).

The next village on the old road, Afándou (the word means "invisible"), is aptly named, for it was completely hidden from marauding pirates and Turks. For that matter, the oldest part of the village, forming the original site, is difficult to spot even from the road. A long stretch of orchards begins at Afándou. Apricots, as well as carpet weaving, are the inhabitants' principal means of livelihood.

RHODES
AEGÉON PÉLAGOS
N
Akrotírio Koúmbournou
Kólpos Triánda
RÓDOS
Rodíni Park
Triánda
Asgouroú
Kremastí
Koskinoú
Filérimos
Paradísion
Thérme Kallithéas
Theológos (Thólos)
Maritsá
Soroní
Dipótama
Faliráki
Fáne
Kallithié
Kalamón
Psínthos
330
Kalavárda
KÁMIROS
PETALOUDES
480
Psínthos
Afándou
Loutáni
Profítis Ilías
Eleoússa
Archípolis
Kolímbia
900
Apóllona
Platánia
551 Eftá Pigés
Tsambíka
Mandríkon
Kámiros Skála
Archángelos
Alimniá
N. Mákri
Akr. Archangélou
Kritinía
Malóna
N. Strongilí
Émbonas
Assouri
397
Makkáris
Gadourás
1215
367
343
Feraklós
Ámartos
Attáviros
Charáki
Tragoússia
Laérma
Kálathos
Ag. Issídoros
Akrotírio Milanós
Akramítis
363
402
Inko
Siánna
LÍNDOS
Lárdos
Monólithos
Istrios
Kontári
Profília
Akr. Mirtiás
Kólpos Lárdou
Asklipiíon
Kólpos Apolakkiás
Apolakkiá
513
Vátion
Koukouliári
Gennádion
Skiádi
Messanagrós
N. Kténia
Lachaniá
Kattaviá
Chochlakas
Agios Pávlos
Plimíri
Akr. Víglos
N. Karavólas
Akrotírio Prassonísi
0 5 10 15 km
0 5 10 miles

Continuing for another seven kilometres, you'll come to KOLÍMBIA. If you look up to your right, you'll see an artificial waterfall. The water flows into irrigation channels that run throughout the area—a system resulting from the new farming methods introduced by the Italians in the 1930s.

Here, a short detour of about five kilometres to the right will bring you to EFTÁ PIGÉS (seven springs), the source of the waterfall. There's a pine-tree shaded restaurant with some tables actually perched on rocks in the middle of a stream. Nearby, at the end of a rugged path (be sure you have rugged shoes, too), is a small man-made lake, fed by the seven springs.

In Afándou, the hidden village, carpet weaving is still an art.

By now, you'll probably have noticed the roadside shrines with their lighted wicks floating in olive oil. Many are dedicated to Greek saints or St. Mary (Panagía). The Greeks on Rhodes have maintained their traditions and beliefs despite centuries of foreign occupation.

South of Kolímbia is a turn-off leading to a sandy and fairly uncrowded beach called TSAMBÍKA, from where a steep climb takes you to MONÍ TSAMBÍKA, a white monastery in a beautiful hilltop setting (see FESTIVALS, page 72). From the top of the peak, there's a commanding view of Mount Attáviros, the highest point on Rhodes.

ARCHÁNGELOS, about six kilometres from Kolímbia, is one of the largest villages on the island and could well be called the capital of the orchard country, for oranges, lemons, figs, olives and grapes grow here in profusion among the sun-drenched white houses. Perched high above the lush vegetation is a 15th-century fortress built by Grand Master Orsini. There's an unusual cemetery in the town with colourfully decorated tombstones.

Archángelos is also well known for its leather peasant boots. They're actually knee-high, but folded down to ankle length. Local women have worn them as protection against snake bites since ancient times. The boots are good looking and comfortable, and if you have time you may want to order a pair.

As you continue to the village of MALÓNA, you'll be surrounded by olive groves dotted with cypress trees. In spring, the rolling countryside is aflame with colourful flowers. Signposts to CHARÁKI lead to a fisherman's village dominated by the castle of FERAKLÓS, which the knights used for prisoners of war as well as for their own misbehavers. After the steep ascent (and descent), you may be glad of a swim from this beach.

Two kilometres beyond the small village of KÁLATHOS, the road forks. To the right is the road leading to Cape Prassonísi, on the southern tip of the island, where there's nothing more than a lighthouse (see page 58). Bear to the left for Líndos.

As you reach the top of this winding road, be prepared for a picture-postcard vista of the ancient port, crowned by an acropolis way above the sea.

Líndos possesses the only natural harbour on the island. It was once one of the most important commercial cities of antiquity, with a population of about 17,000. Today, there are about 700 inhabitants.

Hire your donkey here for the trek up to the acropolis of Líndos.

The layout of the village follows the contours of the hillside and the harbour. Most of the winding streets are just wide enough for donkeys.

There's only one main street. If you follow it from the bus terminus to the base of the acropolis, you'll come to a 15th-century Byzantine church—the **Church of St. Mary** *(Panagía)*. Inside, there are 18th-century frescoes, executed by Gregory of Sími. The floor patterns are made up of black and white sea pebbles. This style of pebble mosaic, typical of certain Aegean islands, is called *chochláki*. You'll see it in houses and courtyards throughout the village.

The main point of interest in Líndos, of course, is the **acropolis**, the site of a 4th-century B.C. temple and medieval fortifications. The latter were added by the Knights of St. John.

You can climb the steps to the acropolis—but be sure to wear comfortable shoes. Women should not attempt it in high heels. Saddled donkeys will take you up the first half of the climb—the steepest part. But no matter how you reach the summit, this is one excursion not to be missed—the acropolis and the view of the harbour are magnificent.

The path to the top from the village will first lead you to a walled platform, bordered by cypress trees. Note the remains of a large stone cistern here, dating back to Byzantine times.

Just before the final ascent you'll come to a 2nd-century B.C. **relief of a Greek warship,** or trireme, carved in the rock. The pedestal in front of the ship once held a bronze statue to a priest of Poseidon, Hagesandros, honoured in 180 B.C. for "his care of the people of Lindos".

Continuing up steep steps, you'll come to the main gate of the fortress, leading to a dark, vaulted hall. (The fortress is open Monday to Saturday, from 9 a.m. until 2.45 p.m. in season; Sundays and holidays, 9 a.m. to 2 p.m.)

A short distance along, you'll see stairs leading to the Commander's Palace and the ruins of a 13th-century Byzantine church. Dominating this part of the acropolis is a double-winged Doric portico, built around 208 B.C. It extends nearly 235 feet. A broad, monumental staircase leads you to a higher terrace containing the foundations of the *propylaea,* or entrance gate, built in the 5th century B.C. The pillars you'll pass as you ascend the staircase were re-erected by Italian archaeologists during this century.

Arriving at the wide *propylaea,* you'll see across the forecourt the surprisingly small **Temple of the Lindian Athena** which is only about 75 feet long and 25 feet wide. It's situated at the edge of a cliff that drops nearly 400 feet to the sea below. The temple

The acropolis of Líndos crowns this peaceful view of Grand Harbour.

dates from the second half of the 4th century B.C. It replaced the temple built during the time of Cleobulos, which was destroyed by fire in 342 B.C.

The temple was built in the Doric style, but unlike most temples of the period, it had columns only at the front and rear. Also unusual is its position. Most Greek temples are sited east to west, but this one runs north to south, so as to fit snugly into the highest point of a triangle formed by the contours of the cliff.

The cult of Athena brings to mind early moon-worship, predating Hellenic civiliza-

Majestic portico of Athena's temple sits on edge of a 400-foot cliff.

tion. But, varying from the usual ceremonial procedure, no fire was permitted inside the Lindian edifice and no animal sacrifices were ever performed by the priestesses here. This fact was established by a chronicle of the temple discovered at the turn of the century and now in the National Museum of Copenhagen.

From the cliffs, you'll look down upon a small, rocky harbour, **Ágios Pávlos Limáni** (St. Paul's Bay). This is where the apostle is said to have disembarked in A.D. 51, en-route to Syria from Ephesus and Troy. The spot is marked by a small white church. St. Paul is generally credited with bringing Christianity to the island.

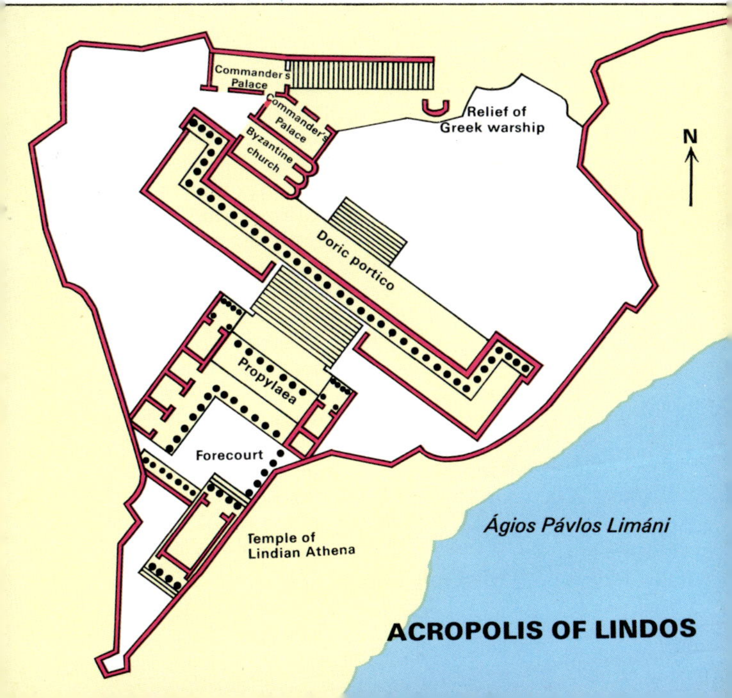

When you return to the village, be sure to take a stroll through the maze of narrow streets. Líndos offers a good sampling of white-washed, cube-shaped, Aegean-style houses. Also, visit the medieval **"captains' houses"**, topped with "captains' rooms", from which ships could be surveyed. Especially noteworthy are the houses of Ioánnis Krékas and Papás Konstandínos. The open doors are an invitation to drop in.

At the south end of the village, you'll see the remains of an ancient wall, which was once part of the gymnasium. Nearby, carved out of rock in the hillside below the acropolis, nestles the ancient theatre with its five aisles.

The Southern Tip

If you feel up to making a complete tour around the island, bear in mind that the road between Kattaviá and Monólithos is still unsurfaced.

Swimmers and sun worshippers should follow the east-coast road to PLIMÍRI where there's a wide cove running to the tip of CAPE VÍGLOS. Between GENNÁDI(ON) and Plimíri there are good sandy stretches of empty beach.

This is a desolate area. In fact KATTAVIÁ the island's southernmost village, could well claim its fuel pump as its most important asset. A rough six-mile track leads from ÁGIOS PÁVLOS to the lonely lighthouse at CAPE PRASSONÍSI.

Heading north, the road from Kattaviá to Monólithos is flat along the windy coast until APOLAKKIÁ where it begins to rise into the mountains. The views are superb.

Make sure the first and second gears of your car are working well and your tires are good. There are no hotels in the area but the odd private room. In desperation you can try the monastery of SKIÁDI—but no guarantee they'll take you in!

In the fields, in the groves, a donkey's a useful thing to have around.

West Coast to Kámiros

The ancient city of Kámiros, abandoned about the time of Christ, is only about 34 kilometres from Rhodes Town. The drive down the west coast, even beyond Kámiros, takes in many spots worthy of side trips, such as Filérimos, Monólithos and the incredible Valley of the Butterflies.

As you leave Rhodes Town heading southwest, you'll come to the village of TRIÁNDA, first settled by Minoans from Crete in the 16th century B.C. During the following century it was probably inundated by tidal waves when Thera (called Santoríni today), the volcanic island near Crete, erupted. Today, the bay of Triánda is the site of some of the island's most popular hotels.

At Triánda, turn off to the left for the steep, winding road to the plateau of **Filérimos** (if you go by public bus, the last part's quite hard going). Iálysos, to use its classical name, was probably first settled by the Phoenicians. Soon after the tidal-wave disaster the Achaeans arrived from the Greek mainland and named the city Achaia. But it wasn't until the Dorians gained control of the region that Iálysos grew into a city-state equalling Líndos and Kámiros in importance.

Perched 880 feet above the sea with a commanding view of the island and the coast, Iályssos had an obvious strategic value. In 1309, the knights launched their attack against the Byzantines from here when they finally seized the island. And ironically, from the very same point, Suleiman the Magnificent surveyed the last stages of his siege in 1522.

Little remains today of the 4th-century Doric temple to Athena and Zeus. The **Church of Our Lady of Filérimos,** originally built in the 14th century, however, has been rebuilt many times. It was restored by the knights, used as a stable by the Turks, restored in the early part of the 20th century by the Italians, destroyed by bombs and then rebuilt in the 1950s.

14th-century (but often rebuilt) Church of Our Lady of Filérimos.

Behind the church is a **monastery,** also restored during the Italian occupation. The cloisters and courtyards are pleasant, quiet places for a stroll. The monastery is still in use, and the monks' cells are distinguished from one another by tiled plaques, each depicting a different flower.

Be sure to visit the underground **chapel-shrine of St. George,** just in front of the temple. The interior walls of this barrel-vaulted chapel are covered with restored 14th- and 15th-century frescoes, depicting scenes from the life of Christ. There's an early Christian cross near the rear, carved in the stone wall. It was discovered under the plaster base of a section of fresco.

Other sites worth a visit on the hill are an 11th-century Byzantine church and the Stations of the Cross, the latter built by the Italians.

If you go down the steps near this latter site, you'll arrive at a 4th-century **Doric fountain.** Once considered a sacred spring, it has since dried up. The Italians restored two of the six columns, which had supported the roof of a portico.

Filérimos is open from 8.45 a.m. to 3 p.m. Monday to Saturday and from 9.30 to 2 on Sundays and holidays.

Continuing along the coastal road towards Kámiros, you'll soon pass through the village of Kremastí.

Kremastí in Greek means "hanging"—the village was so named because the first houses were constructed high up on the side of the hill. The school, near the well-stocked library, is, curiously enough, in the American colonial style. Many residents of Kremastí emigrated to the United States and generously made bequests to the village. Kremastí is well known for its annual festival, held in August, which combines religious ceremonies with folk dancing and sporting events.

Creation of the new airport has radically altered the once attractive farming village of Paradísion, named after nearby Mount Paradísi. Now, the new terminal building sprouts from the village's former market-place.

Past Paradísion, there's a turn-off to the left for Petaloúdes and the **Valley of the Butterflies.** The village of Petaloúdes (meaning "butterflies" in Greek) is seven kilometres beyond that point. The valley is narrow and heavily wooded with pine and storax trees. The storax tree, native to the Turkish Mediterranean coast, contains a resin which faintly smells of vanilla. (The church uses it for making incense.)

It is this same resin that attracts the Quadrina butterfly *(callimorpha quadripunctaria)*. Hundreds of thousands of these butterflies migrate to the valley to mate between June and the end of September.

They're camouflaged a dark brown colour to match the bark of the storax tree and the rocks. When in flight, the full colour of their wings is exposed—black, brown, white and red.

The name "Quadrina" comes from the butterfly's markings four spots and a Roman numeral IV on each wing.

In recent years, the number of Quadrina butterflies, a nocturnal species, has declined sharply, largely because sightseers frightened them into flight during the daytime. It is therefore forbidden to blow whistles, clap hands or otherwise disturb the butterflies while they sleep.

Returning to the car park at the entrance of the valley, you can either continue for five kilometres to PSÍNTHOS, the site of the last battle in 1912 between the invading Italians and the defending Turks, or head back down to the main coastal road.

The village of SORONÍ, on the coastal road, is well known for its annual festival celebrating St. Soúlas (see page 72).

At KALAVÁRDA, about six kilometres from Soroní, the road forks. To the left it leads to 2,600-foot Mount PROFÍTIS ILÍAS. Here in the pine-wooded forest, two mountain lodges, called Élafos (stag) and Elafína (doe), cater to tourists who prefer high altitudes.

But proceeding south to the right, you'll come to a turn-off on the left for **Kámiros** (even if you take the public bus, it's well worth the 20-minute walk from the bus-stop), one of the three major ancient cities on the island already in existence before the city of Rhodes was founded. This point on the island faces directly towards Crete. According to legend Kámiros was founded by Althaemenes, grandson of King Minos of Crete, the mighty ruler of one of the most highly developed ancient civilizations.

Like Iályssos, Kámiros was a flourishing city during the period of the Achaeans in prehistoric times. It continued to prosper under the Dorians and up to the 5th century B.C.

What exists today is an abandoned town in ruins, with traces of its streets and squares still sharply etched in stone. Local guides often compare it to Pompeii, but the analogy is inexact. Pompeii was buried under the hot cinders and ash of a volcano. Kámiros, although damaged by an earthquake, was abandoned and forgotten. It was discovered in 1859, but it wasn't until 1929, under the direction of Italian archaeologists, that full-scale excavations began.

Kámiros was never a fortified city. What now looks like its acropolis was, in fact, the market-place. To the right, as you look up from the entrance, was an extensive water-supply system, including drainage pipes and a large cistern. The Doric **stoa,** or covered walkway, here, built near the cistern, dates from the 6th century. The large portico

Twenty-five centuries have passed since Kámiros was a thriving city.

is 640 feet long. The *stoa* was partially restored by the Italians but, unfortunately, the columns have since toppled over.

Viewing the gentle slope of the site from above, you'll be able to single out the residential area to the right side of the main street, which divides the town. A few re-erected pillars mark the site of a house of the Hellenistic period.

Below, just beyond the entrance, is the sanctuary area, containing the remains of a **Doric temple.** Several of the columns have been put back in place. You'll note stone footprints on the tops of empty pedestals here, where statues once stood. The statues of Kámiros were probably part of the loot plundered by Cassius in 42 B.C. (see page 16).

As you stand at the summit of the excavation site, the woods and grounds you see for a mile or more in all directions were additional districts of ancient Kámiros. But excavation came to a halt when World War II broke out.

Kámiros is open from 8.45 a.m. to 3 p.m. Tuesday to Saturday (closed Monday) and from 9.30 a.m. to 2 p.m. on Sundays and holidays.

KÁMIROS SKÁLA, the last stop on the sea before the road turns inland and into the mountains, is the port from which the caïques of Rhodes carry on trade with the isles of Alimniá and Chálki. In the harbour-side *tavérna* you'll find excellent fresh fish, which is usually prepared on outdoor grills.

If you're adventurous and looking for charming spots well off the tourist track, a few villages further south are worth the inconvenience of the partly unfinished roads.

The first, KRITINÍA, named after its original Cretan settlers, is four and a half kilometres from the sea. Enroute from Kámiros Skála, you'll pass KÁMIROS KASTÉLLO, a fortress built by the knights in the 16th century on the site of an ancient ruin. If you're up to the hike, it's a lovely spot for a picnic—and the view of the sea and the small islands off the coast is delightful.

Continuing past the foothills of Mount Attáviros, you'll come to the village of ÉMBONAS, well known for its women dancers. You'll see them at festivals all over the island. The main means of livelihood here is tobacco and wine, evidenced by vast tobacco fields and vineyards.

From Émbonas, there's a mountain path leading to the top of 3,986-foot MOUNT ATTÁVIROS (see page 94).

Just another 15 kilometres along, you'll come to the village of SIÁNNA. There's a turn-off here to CAPE ARMENISTÍS, a small peninsula near the village.

From Siánna to the small village of MONÓLITHOS you'll be within the shadow of Mount Akramítis.

A few kilometres beyond Monólithos, at the end of a steep and winding road, you'll come to the **castle** of Monóli-

Rhodes' fishermen must go far from shore to catch the really big ones.

thos, perched high upon a rock by the sea (*monólithos* means "a single rock" in Greek). The castle is considered by many to be one of the most beautifully sited in the world. From the top, there's an astonishing sheer drop of 775 feet. There are no guard rails, so be sure to keep back from the edge of the walls as you wander about the site. But that won't hinder your commanding view of the Aegean and the island's coastline. It's a memorable vista.

The castle of Monólithos commands a breath-taking view of the Aegean.

Local Cruises and Boat Trips

If your mind is getting a bit boggled by Greek *bouzoúkia* or medieval knights (if it isn't late nights), you should head down to Mandráki harbour. For here you'll find an array of local ferries and caïques offering a chance to explore the blue Aegean.

SÍMI

There are sailings every morning for Sími and the monastery at Panormítis, only about an hour's trip from Rhodes.

There's a legend that Prometheus (who stole fire from the gods) created man from clay there. Zeus, infuriated, transformed Prometheus into a monkey and, thus, we have the word *simian* and the island's name.

It's a mountainous place with a barren, jagged coast. Sponge fishing is the island's main industry but, because of the danger, a declining one. Nevertheless, you'll still see plenty of sponge fishermen's boats in the capital, the town of SÍMI.

Above the town are some stone pillars, known as the towers of Sími, dating from the days of the Dorian Hexapolis (see page 12). A Byzantine church nearby, built within a Byzantine fort, contains some interesting frescoes.

PANORMÍTIS, a port on the western coast of Sími, is the site of a lovely 18th-century monastery, dedicated to St. Michael. Bells from the monastery's 12th-century chapel will peal in welcome as your boat edges into the bay.

KOS

The island of Kos is served by the Piraeus–Rhodes ferry and by a hydrofoil from Rhodes Town that also takes in Pátmos and Sámos. In the high season, there is an air link, too.

Kos is perhaps best known as the birthplace of Hippocrates, the father of modern medicine. But if you're more of a gourmet than a historian, you'll be interested to know the island is famous for the lettuce that bears its name.

Second largest of the Dodecanese islands, Kos has a population of about 18,000 (half

Greek Orthodox, half Moslem). There's only one important harbour and that's the capital: the town of **Kos.** In 1933, an earthquake destroyed both the town and harbour. But you'll still be able to see the plane tree "so vast that its branches would shade a thousand men" and alleged to be the one under which Hippocrates delivered his lectures and his oath. When you hear this tale, keep in mind that even under the best condi-

Part of Kos' Turkish heritage—the mosque on Platía Eleftherías.

tions, a plane tree's life span rarely exceeds 400 years. But while you're here, why not give in to fantasy? It's a lovely spot, and you can sit by the Turkish fountain and let reality slip away for awhile.

Kos has lovely beaches, a jet airport and an array of hotels. In fact, this prosperous and well-developed island, only three miles from the Turkish coast, merits more than a day-trip.

Start your visit at the **harbour,** where you'll see the town hall and a sea of waterfront restaurants. This area, by the way, is the liveliest spot in town and it's especially colourful in the evenings.

Walk along the palm-tree shaded avenue until you come to the 15th-century **Castle of the Knights.** You can enter the castle along a bridge leading from Platía Platínou. Continuing into the square you'll see the **Mosque of the Loggia.** Note the fine marble staircase leading to the mosque's main entrance. Behind the mosque you'll find the excavations of the *agorá,* or market-place, parts of which date back to the 4th century B.C.

If you have the time, you'll find a visit to the **Asklipiíon** very enlightening. Four kilometres west of town, the road forks off to the left just outside Kos to the Asklipiíon. At this 4th-century B.C. medical sanctuary patients were diagnosed and treated according to the teachings of Hippocrates.

OTHER BOAT TRIPS

There are sailings to other Dodecanese islands—and the choices and departure schedules are quite extensive. For details, inquire at one of the maritime agencies.

Lastly, there are privately owned launches and boats departing daily from Mandráki harbour for coves, beaches and principal tourist attractions such as Líndos.

One of these boats heads down the eastern coast to the sandy beach at Tsambíka, passing Faliráki Beach, Kallithéa, Ladikó and Kolímbia.

If you walk along the harbour in the early evening, you'll see all of these craft moored—their owners trying as hard as they can to sign up passengers for the next morning's departure.

What to Do

Music and Dancing

Tavérnas are where Greeks go to drink wine, eat grilled meat and fish and, above all, to dance and sing. It's also the place where, when spirits start flying, the plates often do, too.

The musician, an indispensable figure in everyday life in Greece.

Music in *tavérnas* is plucked on a *bouzoúki,* a stringed instrument much akin to the mandolin. In many *tavérnas* the *bouzoúki* music blares from a radio or record player of 1930s vintage. It doesn't really matter to the Greeks as long as it's loud.

The roots of authentic Greek music can be traced as far back as the 8th century B.C. when dancing was an essential part of pagan religious rites. Apollo's lyre and the fluted pipe of Pan are today's *bouzoúki* and clarinet, tempered by the chants of the Byzantine church.

During the rule of the Ottoman empire, Greek Orthodox chanters earned a living singing Turkish songs in the houses and palaces of local pashas. The 400 years of Turkish music, heavily influenced by the nasal intonation of Arab wailing, left its mark.

Some *bouzoúki* (or *rebétiko*) songs are now internationally well known thanks to the music of Manos Hadjidakis and Mikis Theodorakis, the singing of Nana Mouskouri and the films of Melina Mercouri. It's likely that this musical art form originated in the slum *tavérnas* and opium dens of

19th-century Piraeus, the port of Athens. The songs dealt with love, poverty and parting from Greece. Today, the lyrics are often based on the themes of modern Greek poetry, inspired by the writings of such men as George Seferis, winner of the Nobel Prize for literature in 1963.

After the Greek army coup in 1967, the songs often told of political suffering and loss of liberty. Theodorakis' protest songs were banned during this period.

When a Greek gets up to dance in a *tavérna,* he's reenacting his heritage and, literally, retracing the steps of

A demure performer at the Traditional Dance Centre.

Principal Festivals and Holy Days

Jan. 1	New Year's Day or St. Basil's Day *(Protochroniá)*. Card games begun the night before and finished on this day test the luck of the Rhodians for the coming year. You might be offered a sprig of basil, a herb named after the saint and a symbol of hospitality.
Jan. 6	Epiphany Day *(ton Theofaníon)*, the day the waters are blessed throughout Greece. In Rhodes Town, a cross blessed by a bishop is tossed into the harbour and children and young men try to retrieve it from the chilly water. The first one to surface with the cross is anointed with oil, blessed and given coins.
Greek Carnival	*Apókries*. For three weeks preceding Lent, there are colourful processions and raucous parties, with the merrymakers donning costumes and masks.
Clean Monday	*Katharí Deftéra,* first day of Orthodox Lent. A day of fasting; some people eat only garlic mashed with potatoes.
Good Friday, Easter	*Megáli Paraskeví, Páscha.* Solemn processions in towns and villages. The celebration of divine liturgy at midnight on Holy Saturday marks the beginning of Easter. When the priest proclaims *Christós Anésti* (Christ is risen), the church courtyard suddenly turns festive—church bells peal, fireworks are set off, and worshippers happily exchange Easter greetings.
July 29 and 30	St. Soúlas Day *(tou Agíou Soúlou)* held near Soroní with lively celebrations that include donkey racing.
Aug. 6 until end of month	Dance festivals in the villages of Maritsá, Kallithiés and Émbonas (famous for its women dancers).
Aug. 15	Assumption Day *(tis Panagías)*. The most renowned festival in the Dodecanese, with dancing and religious processions in Kremastí and Triánda.
Sept. 8	Birth of St. Mary *(Génnisis tis Panagías)*. At Tsambíka, on the eve of this holy day, women in a procession climb the steep hill to the monastery to pray for fertility (see page 52).

Tourists are invited to get in step and join in this lively Greek dance.

his ancestors. He often acts on impulse, dancing because he feels the need to express joy, well-being or sorrow. Dancing has been a criterion of masculine prowess and feminine grace. Traditionally, men danced alone in *tavérnas;* women danced in groups in the village square.

The films "Never on Sunday" and "Zorba the Greek" helped make two traditional dances—the *syrtáki,* a group dance, and the *zebékikos*—popular throughout the world. The *zebékikos,* customarily danced by men, alone or in pairs, depends entirely upon improvised movements inspired by private moods.

What you'll see is a bewildering display of agility and emotion. But always remember that the Greek dances for himself, his need, his pleasure. Don't interrupt him. He dances because he likes it.

Other common Greek dances are the *kalamatianós,* a circle dance; the *tsakónikos;* the *tsámikos,* a handkerchief dance; the *chasápikos,* known as the butchers' dance, and the *naftikós,* the sailors' dance.

From May to October, you can see traditional dances performed in national and regional costumes at the Traditional Dances Center near Platía Androníkou (beside the Turkish Baths) in the Old Town, home of the Nelly Dimoglou Dance Company, a 40-member troupe dedicated to preserving Greece's folk traditions.

Nightlife

In good weather, you can spend a few delightful hours in the Municipal Gardens at the **Son et Lumière** show. From April to October there are three performances nightly except Sunday—in different languages—retelling the siege of Suleiman the Magnificent.

The sounds of rock alternate with *bouzoúki* music in the **nightclubs** and **discotheques** in Rhodes Town. Most of the larger hotels outside town also have clubs.

The **casino** in the Grand Hotel in Rhodes Town was opened by a group headed by Baron von Richthofen, nephew of the World War I flying ace. In the early days, the croupiers were flown in from Baden-Baden, Germany.

You can try your luck at roulette, black-jack, chemin-de-fer and baccarat. You need your passport to get in. Blue jeans are not allowed, men must wear a shirt with collar.

Foreign **films** are shown in the original language with Greek subtitles.

Illuminated Palace of the Grand Masters seen from Mandráki.

Museums

The Archaeological Museum of Rhodes (*archeologikó mousío*—see page 27) in the Knights' Hospital on Ippotón. Open from 8 a.m. to 7 p.m. (till 6 p.m. on Sundays), closed on Tuesdays.

The Museum of Decorative Arts on Platía Argirokástrou, housed in what is thought to have been the arsenal, has a collection of well-preserved Rhodian costumes, embroidery, ceramics and other decorative folk art. A reconstruction of a room in a Rhodian house shows how these items were used.

Potential shoppers are advised to study these authentic displays for ideas before buying anything to take home. Open Monday, Wednesday and Friday from 9 a.m. to 1 p.m.

The Art Gallery *(pinakothíki)* on the upper floor of the Ionian and Popular Bank on Platía Símis displays paintings by local artists of local scenes worth looking at. Open Monday to Saturday from 7.30 a.m. to 3 p.m., and Tuesday to Friday from 5 to 8 p.m., closed on Sundays.

Shopping

When the Dodecanese Islands were united with Greece in 1947, they were granted special low duty privileges. As a result, foreign products such as cloth, woollen fabrics, jewelry, furs and whisky are cheaper here than in their country of origin (the local sales tax is also avoided). Any goods imported from Athens, however, bear taxes and the increased cost of shipping and are more expensive than on mainland Greece.

Prices are fixed in the major shops and fashionable boutiques—and on most brand-name goods. There's more freedom for manœuvre—if you're not overpowered by the range of choice—in the smaller, near medieval-size shops on Sokrátous in the Old Town. It's worth walking the whole length of this street before buying anything—even though it does start at sea level and rise steeply. There are plenty of cafes in the middle and at the top if you need a break—restaurants too if you decide to shop in the cool of the evening rather than the heat of the day. It's worth spending time looking for exactly what you want. Prices and quality vary and at least half the fun of shopping is examining the goods. Nobody will mind if you finger it, tap it, turn it upside down (and for clothing, inside out).

...and Keep in Mind

By and large, prices in Greece are lower than in other European countries. Even in high-quality items, you'll find good buys. After scouting around the shops, you'll probably discover that it's worth paying a little more for the best. Be on the lookout for tourist traps—their wares may look tempting, but they might not make it home in one piece.

Shopping Hours

The shopping hours in Rhodes are from 8.30 a.m. to 1 p.m. and from 5 to 8.30 p.m. Most shops close on Saturday afternoon, with the exception of grocers', barbers' and hairdressers', which are closed on Wednesday afternoon.

Best Buys

At the top of the list are gold and silver jewellery, British fabrics and tailor-made clothes, fur coats and hats. Cashmere, Harris tweed, worsteds, camel's hair—in fact, most top-quality British fabrics—are sold at close to duty-free prices. There are about 300 tailor's shops in Rhodes. They'll cut, fit and deliver a suit or dress in no time at all. The clothes should be ready to wear in about three days.

Ancient designs are painstakingly reproduced in a potter's workshop.

Furs, especially domestic stone marten, are among the best shopping buys in Greece. In Rhodes the prices are even more tempting. Some fur coats are made from left-over pieces of pelt, artfully sewn together. The technique is a Greek speciality.

The more than 80 furriers in Rhodes carry a wide selection of furs including stone marten, red fox, wolf (popular with men), rabbit and doeskin. The coats are hand-stitched in workshops on the island and, with the required three fittings, will take about a week for delivery.

When you order custom-tailored clothing, keep in mind that the tailor may not have read the latest fashion journals. Therefore, it's wise to select the style you want in advance, and then carefully explain your ideas to the tailor.

Shoes for men and women—especially top-quality models made for export—are an excellent buy. Shop around. You'll find shoes made here that will wind up in Paris shop windows at twice the price.

Jewelry is generally fashioned of silver and 18-carat gold. Semi-precious stones are imported from Italy (at low duty rates) and made into rings, brooches, necklaces and other jewelry in the local silver- and goldsmith's shops.

The price of gold and silver fluctuates on the world market, but since labour on the island is relatively inexpensive, jewelry is, too.

Imported liquor isn't entirely duty free, but it's nevertheless quite reasonable.

Other Good Buys

Pottery from Líndos is world famous for its decorative beauty. The brightly coloured plates (note those with ship, fish and floral patterns) make excellent gifts and souvenirs, and they're good buys. You'll find ceramic factories all over the island, and it's wise to visit one to get a good idea of the variety and price. You can also buy directly from the factories.

Handmade lace is another bargain from Líndos. Before you buy these handicrafts, have a look around the Museum of Decorative Arts in the Old Town (see page 75). Again, it will give you a better idea of what you're buying.

Late-night shopping outside the medieval walls by the light of an oil lamp.

Olive-wood salad bowls, carving boards, mortars and pestles and bracelets are also worth looking for. If you can spare the time, it's a good idea to make your purchases at a factory.

Handmade leather peasant boots from the village of Archángelos (see page 53) can also be purchased in the Old Town. They're rugged yet comfortable and are becoming very popular.

Also Worth Considering

The sprawling streets and passageways of the Old Town provide an amusing place to browse, and its shops are crammed full of inexpensive items. While fighting your way through the noisy crowd, high-pressure merchants and overladen street stalls, look for Turkish brass and copper pots, long-handled Turkish coffee pots *(bríkia)* and *souvlákia* skewers. Here and in other parts of town, you'll also find *kombolóïa,* the famous Greek worry beads, Greek shoulder bags and sponges. (There are hordes of sponge salesmen along the harbour.)

Bootmaker in Archángelos turns out traditional Rhodian footwear.

Wining and Dining

When it comes to wining and dining in Greece, you owe it to yourself to be a bit adventuresome. It's easy to pass over some typical Greek menu selections without further thought. But don't. Give even the more exotic specialities a try, such as grilled octopus, goat's milk cheese steeped in brine, lemon soup and resin-flavoured wine. You probably won't regret the chance you took.

There are so many restaurants and *tavérnas* on Rhodes, you might want to think twice about taking full board at your hotel. Much of the food at the more expensive hotels tends to have a continental influence and the menu might read a bit like the ones you've read on other holidays—or in your home town.

You'll find the method of making your selection in a restaurant *(estiatórion)* and *tavérna* an interesting and amusing experience. For it's Greek practice for the customer to enter the kitchen and inspect the array of cooking pots—even ask to look in the refrigerator—to get an idea of the day's menu. You can take all the time you need—smelling the simmering specialities of the day—and order anything which catches your fancy. Don't worry about the obvious language problem. You can always point while you're standing in front of the rows of pots and pans. If you ask for *olígo* of anything (a little), you'll be served a half-portion.

Dishes should be ordered for their diversity and above all to share; often all the serving dishes are placed on the table, and the customer is expected to help himself. If you think you might feel a bit uncomfortable wandering about the kitchen to make your selection, you'll be consoled to know that in most cases, menus are written in one or more European languages (English, French, German and Swedish) as well as Greek. In any case, Greek letters will be transcribed in the Latin alphabet.

Keep in mind that in most Greek restaurants you won't dine elegantly. The emphasis is on honest cooking and an informal atmosphere.

Restaurants open at noon, but don't get crowded until

2 p.m. Although dinner is served from 8 p.m., most Greeks eat much later. You'll find the locals meeting at a *kafenío* (café) for a before-dinner drink as late as 9 p.m. Hotels try to maintain earlier meal times to accommodate northern habits, but you're likely to fall into step quickly with the local easy-going way of life.

All eating establishments (with the exception of those in the luxury class) are price-controlled according to category. The service charge is included in the bill. As a rule, you're expected to leave a bit extra for the waiter. If a youngster brings iced water or an ashtray, or cleans off the table, it's customary to hand him a few drachmas as you leave.

Greek Specialities

Greece shares a common bond with the whole Mediterranean region in its style of cooking, although there has been a Turkish and Arab influence. On Rhodes, the Turkish influence is especially pronounced. The ingredients used most often to season dishes are olive oil, tomatoes, lemon, onion, garlic and cheese.

Here's a selection of dishes you're likely to find in most restaurants,* no matter what their category:

Soúpa avgolémono: the best known Greek soup, made with chicken or meat stock, eggs and rice, flavoured with lemon juice. It has a delightfully refreshing flavour and is often served just before the last course. The Greeks feel it helps settle the stomach. A sauce made from the same ingredients is often used to flavour other dishes such as hot *dolmádes* and stuffed aubergines.

Dzadzíki: a yoghurt dip with thinly sliced cucumbers and flavoured with garlic. It's served cold and usually with other *mezédes* (snacks) such as *taramosaláta, dolmádes* and *keftédes.*

Taramosaláta: a spread made with *taramá* (grey mullet roe); the roe along with mashed potatoes, moistened bread, olive oil and lemon juice are beaten into a smooth spread. Greeks like to dip pieces of bread into the mixture to eat as an appetizer. It

* For a comprehensive glossary of Greek wining and dining terms, ask your bookshop for the Berlitz EUROPEAN MENU READER.

may also be served on lettuce as a salad.

Dolmádes: grape leaves stuffed with minced meat (usually lamb) and rice and seasoned with wine, grated onion and herbs. They're made in many Middle-Eastern countries; in Greece they're often served hot with an *avgolémono* sauce.

Keftédes: meat balls, usually made with minced beef and lamb and flavoured with grated onion, cinnamon, crushed mint leaves, oregano and wine. They're baked or deep-fried in oil and served with a sauce.

Moussaká: one of the best known and popular Greek dishes. The basic ingredients are sliced aubergine and minced meat. Alternate layers of both are baked with a bechamel sauce and grated cheese.

Kolokithia gemistá me rízi ke kimá: marrow (zucchini) stuffed with rice and minced meat.

Kotópoulo vrastó: boiled chicken with noodles or rice.

Kotópoulo psitó (sti soúvla): (spit-roasted) chicken.

Arní psitó: roast lamb.

Fish is surprisingly expensive, because fishermen have to travel further and further from the island for a worthwhile catch. It's wise to go into the kitchen to see what fish are available. Your choice will be weighed before your eyes, and you actually pay by the kilo.

It is usually grilled or fried, basted with oil and served with oil and lemon juice.

The following are the more common fish and seafood from local waters:

Astakós: spiny lobster, often served with oil and lemon sauce or garlic mayonnaise.

Barboúni: red mullet, considered by Greeks to be the best of all the local fish. It's also the most expensive; usually dusted with flour and fried.

Chtapódi: octopus; usually cut in slices and fried or boiled.

Fagrí: sea bream, it's best baked.

Garídes: prawns.

Glóssa: sole (not as large as the ocean variety).

Kalamaráki: squid.

Kéfalos: grey mullet.

Lithríni: spotted bream.

Marídes: similar to the Atlantic sprat.

Don't miss the delicious Greek "village" salads *(saláta choriátiki),* made with sliced cucumbers, tomatoes, green

VODKA
3.00 W.G.
PROOF
MORETTI BIRRA FRIULANA
MA-ΠΟ-ΛΕ

peppers, onions, radishes, olives and topped with *féta,* a Greek cheese made from sheep's milk. You can also order any of these salad vegetables singly, if you prefer. In most *tavérnas,* you can prepare your own—just the way you like it. You'll see people dousing their salads with lots of oil—in typical Greek style.

One last word on restaurant dining: fruit from the islands is a real delight. *Pepóni* (a melon with a taste somewhere between cantaloupe and honey dew) and *karpoúzi* (water-melon) are mouth-watering. So are the peaches, oranges, figs (August figs are the best) and seedless grapes. You can order a bowl of mixed fruit for any number of people—and it will arrive at your table ready to eat, peeled and cut.

Exotic grilled octopus tastes far better than it actually looks.

Snacks

The informality of Greek eating habits helps make life easier for busy tourists on the run. You'll find tasty and inexpensive snacks at a *psistariá* (with grilled specialities) in Rhodes Town and the larger villages. Ask for *souvlákia,* pieces of veal, lamb or pork and vegetables grilled on a skewer *(soúvla); giros,* or *donér kebáb,* is a large piece of meat cooked on a vertical spit and carved into slices. Also try *souvláki me pítta,* grilled meat, tomatoes, peppers and onions in a round, flat bun *(pítta).*

For less spicy treats, head for a *galaktopolío,* a dairy counter selling items such as yoghurt, milk, butter, pastries and one of the island's specialities—*rizógalo.* This is chilled rice pudding, deliciously flavoured with lemon juice and cinnamon. Another popular snack you'll find here is *tirópitta,* a cheese-filled pastry.

These little shops are handy for a do-it-yourself Greek-style breakfast, too. Buy some bread, yoghurt and honey (try a little honey on the yoghurt) and head for a nearby café in the warm rays of the morning sun.

Cafés

A popular evening pastime in Rhodes is café- and restaurant-hopping. A delightful spot for aperitifs and hors d'œuvre in the early evening is Mandráki harbour. Then, after dinner, perhaps by the harbour or in town, it's pleasant to take coffee or drinks in a café or *tavérna* in yet another part of town, such as the Old Town or the Turkish quarter.

Before dinner, try *oúzo,* the national aperitif. This is a clear, aniseed-flavoured spirit, reminiscent of French *pastis*

Turkish coffee and the morning paper—two "musts" for every Greek.

or Turkish *rakí*. It's usually mixed with cold water (it turns a milky colour when water is added), but you can also have it neat, or straight *(skéto)*, or on the rocks *(me págo)*. Drink *oúzo* in moderation. It has quite a kick, and you won't see Greeks drinking it without some sort of snack.

You'll be served a small plate of *mezédes* with it, usually cheese, olives, tomatoes, *taramosaláta* and slices of fried octopus. The *mezédes* will vary according to the type of café you select.

Keep in mind that you're on a duty-free island, so if you prefer whisky or gin (tonic is available), the price will be reasonable. The Greeks make several very good vermouths. Cinzano is also produced locally, under licence.

If you prefer something non-alcoholic, you'll find most cafés have a good selection. An excellent soft drink is *vissináda*, made from the juice of sour cherries. It comes bottled, but for a special treat, ask for a small dish of thick cherry syrup and spoon it into a glass of cold water. You'll find bottled orange drinks, *portokaláda*, and lemon drinks, *lemonáda*, very satisfying, too. Other popular refreshers are *Tamtam*, a kind of cola drink, and *Ivi*, tinned orange juice.

Greek coffee (actually Turkish in origin) is boiled to order in a long-handled copper or aluminium pot called a *bríki* and poured, grounds and all, into your cup. Ask for *éna varý glikó* for sweet coffee; *éna métrio*, medium, or *éna skéto*, bitter (without sugar). When the coffee is served, wait a few minutes before sipping it, so the grounds will settle. Don't be surprised when the waiter brings you a glass of water with your coffee. The two are traditionally served together.

By your second day on Rhodes, you'll probably be desperate for a cup of coffee, home-style. Your best bet is instant coffee; it's referred to everywhere as *nes*. Some of the better cafés also serve espresso, and if you look around the New Town, you'll find Scandinavian restaurants featuring their own coffee.

Iced coffee, *frappé*, is a popular hot-weather drink.

As for tea, don't expect it served in a pot, British style. The water is good and hot, but you're more than likely to find a tea bag floating in it.

Some cafés also serve pastries. And a tea shop *(zacharoplastío)*, often fronted with a pleasant terrace, has mouth-watering specialities. Several sweets are made of *fíllo,* flaky, paper-thin pastry. The best known is *baklavá,* a pastry made of *fíllo,* filled with chopped almonds and walnuts and steeped in honey or syrup. *Kataïfi* may look like shredded-wheat breakfast food, but the similarity stops there. It, too, is made of *fíllo* and honey.

Ice-cream is popular in Greece, and it's excellent. If you're in the mood for a few scoops of your favourite flavour, an ice-cream sundae or other ice-cream concoctions, head for a *kafenío* or *zacharoplastío*. For something less filling, try a *granita,* scoops of home-made water ice, or sherbet.

Wines and Spirits

The first time you sip a glass of *retsína,* the classic Greek white wine, you'll probably think the waiter has misunderstood your order. This tangy wine is flavoured with resin, giving it a slight turpentine-like taste. You may be surprised, but don't be alarmed. The Greeks have been drinking *retsína*—and enjoying it—since ancient times.

Greek wines were originally transported and stored in pine-wood casks, sealed with resin. In later years, when vats and bottles replaced the casks, the Greeks continued to resinate their wines to preserve the memory of the ancient flavour.

Try a glass with your meal. You might just acquire a taste for it before too long. The Greeks say it rarely causes hangovers and helps to digest rich, oily foods.

If you find it's taking you longer than you expected to acquire a taste for *retsína,* you'll find a good selection of un-resinated wines *(aretsínoto krasí)* on Rhodes. *Deméstícha,* available as white or red, is both popular and inexpensive. *Sánta Hélena* and *Pallíni* are pleasant, dry whites. Among the dependable Greek reds are *Náoussa* and *Sánta Láoura*.

Good wines from Rhodes are *Lindos Blanc Sec* and *Grand Maître* (both white) and *Chevalier de Rhodes,* probably the best local red. It's sometimes referred to as "the wine the Knights used to drink".

You may find Greek red wines a bit heavy. If so, try lighter bodied rosés.

Greek beer *(bíra)* has German origins and is excellent. Many well-known European breweries bottle beer in Greece.

Greek brandy is sweet and, although locally known as *cognac,* it cannot be compared to the famed French brandy. It is, nevertheless, quite agreeable. *Metaxá* is the best known brand; *Kambá* is a little drier.

The view and fresh breeze can only enhance the taste of the seafood.

Sports and Outdoor Activities

Even if the myth about the sun god Helios choosing Rhodes as his place in the sun is a bit hard to believe, you'll believe everything else you've heard about Rhodes' warm, sunny climate as soon as you step off your plane. In fact, on Rhodes you'll probably do as the Rhodians do—and spend most of your time outdoors.

The choice of recreational activities is excellent—ranging from underwater swimming and snorkelling to hiking to the peak of Mount Attáviros.

BOATING AND SAILING

Mandráki harbour is the hub for yacht, sailing-boats and motorboat rentals. For smaller sailing-boats, try the Rhodes Yachting Club, near the Elli Beach Club. But keep in mind that the local and unpredictable *meltémi,* or north wind, can make sailing in small boats very tricky. So when the winds blow and the waves rise, it might be best to wait for a calmer sea-going day.

Pedalos are small two-seater craft propelled by a foot-driven water wheel. They're just the thing for a leisurely trip around harbours and coves. You'll find them for hire on beaches along the east coast, where the water is less choppy.

SKIN-DIVING

Bear in mind, before you put on your wet suit, that it's forbidden to tamper with or remove any archaeological remains from the sea bed. And if you think you've spotted a relic, you're expected to report it to the authorities.

Spear fishing, on the other hand, is a very popular sport here. You won't need a permit, but you won't be allowed within 100 yards of public beaches either. And just be sure when you take aim that the fish weighs more than 150 grams (5 oz.).

Snorkellers will find plenty of colourful fish swimming about in the warm, blue Aegean—and scores of hermit crabs capering among the rocks and pebbles along the bottom.

You can hire a boat and take in the coastal sights along Kallithéa Bay.

WATER-SKIING

Water-ski enthusiasts should make for the island's eastern coast, where the sea and wind are calmer. Try Faliráki beach, Líndos or some of the hotels. Prices vary with the location and size of the boat. Ask at your hotel desk.

SWIMMING

With over 300 days of sunshine and clear skies a year, it's easy to understand why Rhodes' most popular and available sport is swimming. The eastern coast has long stretches of superb beaches.

The beach of Faliráki, fewer than 20 kilometres south of Rhodes Town, is long and sandy. It slopes gently out to the sea and is ideal for children. It's also the most popular and therefore the most crowded. If you prefer a quieter setting, continue down the beach in a southerly direction, until you come to a sheltered and normally uncrowded bay.

There are plenty of seaside amenities at Faliráki, including restaurants with rooms to let, changing cabins, showers, deck-chairs and parasols. It's a good spot for water-skiing too. During the summer, there are frequent bus services from Rhodes Town (see page 104).

Tsambíka Beach, looking out on to the bay of Archángelos, and Stregéna (reached by a fairly long walk from the road) are superb. And the long pebble stretch of beach between Charáki and Cape Milianós (about four miles) is not only one of the best swimming locales on the island, it's also reasonably deserted.

The beach around the Bay of Líndos is wide and sandy—and the water is beautifully clear. Its setting is idyllic, with the charming fishermen's village nearby and the spectacular acropolis and Temple of Athena towering high above. There are changing facilities, showers and three restaurants on the cove. But, like Faliráki, it might be crowded.

You might prefer to continue to Lárdos Bay on the south side of the Lindian peninsula, where the long, sand-dune dotted beach seems almost undiscovered.

From the Bay of Lárdos, there's a long, 14-mile stretch of beach running almost continously to Cape Víglos.

A pleasant spot on the east coast within easy cycling distance of Rhodes Town (it's only about 10 kilometres) is Kallithéa Spa. The spa has seen better days, but the small bay is delightful for swimming (see page 49).

To get a good picture in your mind of the swimming possibilitites on the eastern coast, you might want to cruise by the beaches on an excursion boat. You can easily catch a caïque at Mandráki harbour (see page 69).

Finding a good place to swim on the western coast is another story. The main problem here is the wind and choppy seas. The beaches are generally pebbly and not as accessible. South of Kámiros, the coast is rocky and craggy.

The bay at Kámiros, however, is an exception. The beach here is excellent, and when the sea is calm, you can swim without risk.

If you're looking for a place to spread your beach towel in Rhodes Town, make your way to the Elli Beach Club or the beaches adjoining it. You'll have to pay a small fee there to use the changing rooms and shower. Also nearby are the beaches on the Bay of Triánda. Aktí Miaoúli and Aktí Kanári are closest to Rhodes Town.

Some of the hotels on the western coast near Rhodes Town have swimming pools that are open to the public. If you prefer your sunning and swimming "resort hotel style", try one of the big, new hotels outside town in the direction of Ixiá. It's wise to find out first if the pool is open to visitors.

NB: Sunbathing and swimming in the nude are now considered punishable offences.

Sheltered from strong winds, the east coast offers attractive beaches.

HIKING

You probably didn't come to Rhodes to climb nearly 4,000 feet to the summit of Mount Attáviros, but if you'd like to see the scant remains of a Hellenistic temple of the god Zeus and enjoy the most extensive view of the island, head for the village of Émbonas—about 60 kilometres from Rhodes Town. The villagers will direct you to the mountain path. (You'll find it tricky to locate on your own.) The ascent takes about three hours and should not be attempted alone. In Émbonas, you can arrange to spend the night in private rooms.

GOLF

There's an 18-hole golf course at Afándou, about 22 kilometres from Rhodes Town (see page 50). Professional coaching is available.

The island's eastern coast is the place to go for water-skiing.

TENNIS

Many of the island's hotels have courts open to the public and tennis equipment can often be rented on the spot. Ask your own hotel desk-clerk to help you find a court near the hotel and reserve a time.

HUNTING

There are plenty of deer running wild in the less populous parts of the island. And a stag is even the symbol of Rhodes (see page 43). But if you see one when you're hunting, point your rifle in the other direction. They're protected by law and are not to be harmed in any way.

The hunting season runs from August 25 to March 10 for most game. The season on migratory birds is from August 25 to September 30 and on rabbits and partridge from November 1 to January 10.

Keep in mind that game is not over-abundant on the island (see page 96).

A licence is required. Apply to the Rodia Elafos Club in town.

FLORA

According to one of the many legends associated with the creation of Rhodes, Helios asked Aphrodite to be the island's patron-goddess. She bestowed upon it her symbol, the rose, and made it grow in profusion. Some people still refer to Rhodes as Rose Island.

The word *ródon* from which the name "Rhodes" was derived, probably refers to a rose rather than to the nymph Rhodon mentioned in another legend. There's further confusion about the kind of "rose" the legend refers to. Among the possibilities are the pomegranate flower, the hibiscus, oleander and the cistus, or rock rose.

In any case, all of these flowers bloom profusely in the spring, along with bougainvillea, jasmine, honeysuckle, cyclamen and mimosa. You'll also see spring poppies, flaming scarlet amidst fields of grain, and daisies growing in the shade of fig trees.

Incidentally, be sure to try the delicious honey on Rhodes. People have been praising the honey from the Dodecanese Islands since ancient times.

The trees you'll see most frequently here are the olive, Aleppo pine, citrus (orange, lemons and mandarine), almond, shrub oak, fig and cypress—all typical Mediterranean species.

Olive and citrus trees were brought to the shores of the Mediterranean from the Orient centuries ago, and today, the cultivated olive tree is by far the most valuable tree around.

If you come to Rhodes during the winter months, you'll probably notice the heavy scent of the orange and lemon blossoms in the air. By summer, the oranges are all over the ground in the orchards. The tangy taste of freshly picked oranges is a special treat. But avoid eating the bitter ones (Seville type), destined for the marmalade pot. The delicate white flower is used to scent some colognes.

According to legend, the purple flowers on the Judas tree, which appear in March or April before the leaves, were once pale. After Judas hanged himself, the blooms blushed dark with shame.

Another biblical allusion: the leathery pods of the carob tree, Rhodians assert, were the locusts eaten by John the Baptist. They're used today as cattle fodder.

What looks like a type of cactus growing all over the countryside is actually prickly pear. Its fruit, sometimes called barbary fig, is edible if you can get at it. Some say it was brought to Europe from South America by Christopher Columbus. Today, Rhodians often use the spiny plant as a hedge to contain animals.

FAUNA

Apart from the famous Rhodian deer, you'll find marten, fox, hare, rabbits, badgers and hedgehogs scurrying about in the less populous areas. Greek marten fur is well known and is an especially good buy on Rhodes (see page 78).

If you hear people speak of the "Rhodes Dragon", you needn't have to worry about carrying a sword in your belt when you venture into the country. It's simply a crested green lizard *(agama stellio)*, sometimes reaching a length of 18 inches. It's very quick but harmless.

BLUEPRINT for a Perfect Trip

How to Get There

Because of the complexity and variability of the many fares, you should ask the advice of an informed travel agent well before your departure.

BY AIR

Scheduled Flights

From London: Regular, non-stop flights operate to Athens from London and provincial airports. From Athens, there are frequent connections to Rhodes, a trip of less than one hour.

From North America: there are no non-stop services to Rhodes. All flights are routed via Athens (or a European gateway city). The air trip from Athens to Rhodes takes about one hour. There are several flights a day in the summer months, fewer in winter.

Special excursion fares are available. If you can plan and pay far enough in advance, APEX (advance purchase excursion) or ABC (advance booking charter) fares can mean even greater savings.

Charter Flights and Package Tours

From North America: ABC flights cost less than APEX, but go to fewer destinations. These flights on chartered aircraft are open to all, though tickets must be purchased several weeks in advance.

Club charters, cheaper still, require that you be a member of the organization for a least six months before departure.

From the British Isles: a large number of tour operators offer holidays in Rhodes in both their summer and winter programmes. Prices vary enormously, depending on whether the package incorporates flight by scheduled or charter airline and upon the standard of hotel accommodation.

BY SEA

International sea routes connect Rhodes with Turkey, Cyprus, Israel and Egypt. Vessels operating on these itineraries are generally large passenger ships, many equipped to carry cars. Your travel agent or the Greek National Tourist Organization will have the latest information. In addition, car ferries and passenger boats operate between Rhodes and Piraeus—at least one per day, except on Sundays. Some ferries to Rhodes make several stops along the way but the *f/b Rodos* operates direct and completes the run Piraeus–Rhodes in about 12 hours.

Prices on these island boats are reasonable; they're scaled for the Greek pocket. Deck class can be an adventure in itself. You could end up spending the evening with *bouzoúki* dancers or sharing sleeping space with cats and chickens.

BY ROAD

There's a wide variety of sea-land routes available between the U.K. and Rhodes. It is certainly not the quickest or most comfortable way of reaching Rhodes, nor is it likely to be the cheapest unless several people are sharing a car. Allow at least four to five days. Cross-Channel ferry and hovercraft space is very much in demand in summer. The most direct route to Athens via Frankfurt–Munich–Graz (Austria)–Belgrade–Skopje (Yugoslavia) and on to Athens—approximately 2,000 miles from the channel ports. The route via Italy and the Ancona–Patras ferry is easier.

Alternatively, some coach operators offer excursions from London and Continental Europe to Athens in summer.

Crossing the Channel: during the summer, when ferry space is at a premium, be sure you have a firm reservation. The principal car-ferry routes link Dover and Folkestone with Calais, Boulogne and Dieppe; also Weymouth–Cherbourg, Plymouth–Roscoff; and Rosslare, Ireland, with Le Havre and Cherbourg.

The hovercraft service between Dover and Calais takes about 35 minutes.

BY RAIL

It is possible to travel from London to Greece by train, but be prepared for a long trip. From Paris, there are two main routes (although a number of variations are possible): the cheaper route is via Simplon, Venice, Ljubljana, Belgrade and Salonica. The other, more expensive, route goes via Bologna, Brindisi and Patras (the fare includes ferry crossing Brindisi–Patras).

Anyone under 26 years of age can purchase an *Inter-Rail* card which allows one month's unlimited second-class travel. The *Rail Europ S* card, obtainable before departure only, entitles senior citizens to purchase train tickets for European destinations at reduced prices. People living outside Europe and North Africa can purchase a *Eurail-pass* for unlimited rail travel in 16 European countries, including Greece. This pass must be obtained before leaving home.

When to Go

Rhodes enjoys a good climate throughout the year, with the sun hottest from July to September. January and February are the coolest months, and January is also the rainiest.

Weather statistics can be misleading, however, since even in midsummer you may be unlucky enough to have bad weather. So go prepared with clothing to match almost any occasion.

	J	F	M	A	M	J	J	A	S	O	N	D
Air temperature												
°F	54	54	55	63	70	77	81	82	78	68	61	55
°C	12	12	13	17	21	25	27	28	25	20	16	13
Water temperature												
°F	59	57	59	63	66	72	75	77	75	73	66	61
°C	15	14	15	17	19	22	24	25	24	23	19	16
Rainy days	17	12	11	7	5	1	1	1	3	8	12	16

All figures shown are approximate monthly averages.

Planning Your Budget

To give you an idea of what to expect, here are some average prices in Greek drachmas. However, all prices must be regarded as *approximate*, as they rise inexorably, in particular at the beginning of each tourist season.

Airport transfer. Bus to Rhodes Town 200 drs., taxi 1,500 drs.

Bicycle and motorscooter rental. Bicycles 800–1,500 drs. per day, motorscooters 3,000–3,500 drs. per day.

Buses. Rhodes Town to Líndos 650 drs., to Kallithea 190 drs.

Car Hire (July–October). *Fiat Panda* 8,500 drs. per day plus 48 drs. per km, 12,000 per day unlimited mileage. *Suzuki Jeep* 15,000 drs. plus 55 drs. per km, 18,000 per day with unlimited mileage. All prices include insurance and 13% VAT.

Cigarettes. Greek brands 220–350 drs. per packet of 20, foreign brands 450 drs.

Entertainment. *Bouzoúki* evening, including drink 2,000–4,000, including food 5,000 drs., discotheque (admission and first drink) 2,000–2,500 drs.

Hairdressers. *Woman's* haircut 1,700–3,000 drs., shampoo and set 1,700–2,200 drs. *Man's* haircut 1,700–3,000 drs. (Add 16% VAT.)

Hotels (double room with bath per night, high season, breakfast and all taxes included). De Luxe and Class A prices are for half-board. De luxe 25,000–35,000 drs., Class A 20,000–25,000 drs., Class B 12,000–15,000 drs., Class C 9,000–12,000 drs., Class D 6,000–7,000 drs.

Meals and drinks. Continental breakfast 700–1,100 drs., lunch or dinner in fairly good establishment 2,500–7,000 drs., beer 500–700 drs., coffee 200–400 drs., soft drink 280–300 drs., Greek brandy (three stars) 500–600 drs.

Shopping bag. Ready-made salads (250 g) tuna 454 drs., taramasalata 284 drs., aubergine 413 drs., 500 g feta cheese 550–650 drs., 100 g salami 210 drs., 6 eggs 190 drs., 500 g tin black olives 500 drs., 1 kg oranges 200–300 drs., melon 300–350 drs. per kg, 1,5 litre mineral water 90–190 drs.

Sports. Dinghy 1,800–2,000 drs. per hour. Water-skiing 2,800 drs. for 10 minutes. Tennis 2,500–2,900 drs. per couple per hour.

An A–Z Summary of Practical Information and Facts

Listed after most main entries is an appropriate Greek translation, usually in the singular. You'll find this vocabulary useful when asking for information or assistance.

A star (*) following an entry indicates that relevant prices are to be found on page 101.

A **AIRPORT** *(aerodrómio).* All incoming flights land at the international airport about 15 kilometres from Rhodes Town. Formalities on arrival or departure are kept to a minimum and suitcases are only spot-checked. Porters are available to carry bags to the taxi rank. Luggage of those on package tours is often transferred to waiting coaches without customs inspection. These special buses conveniently drop you off at your hotel.

Some public buses pass through the airport on their way to or from Rhodes, and there is a bus station 200 metres outside the airport.

For flight details contact the Olympic Airways Office:

9, Ieroú Lóchou, Rhodes Town, tel. 24 571 (reservations 24 555).

Porter!	**Achthofóre!**
Where's the bus for...?	**Pou íne to leoforío giá...?**

ALPHABET and LANGUAGE. The Greek alphabet needn't be a mystery to you. The table below lists the Greek letters in their capital and small forms, followed by the letters they correspond to in English. In cases where there are various possibilities, we give pronunciation examples.

Unfortunately, there's still no consistency in the way the Greeks themselves transcribe their language. Thus, the word *ágios* (saint) is very often spelt *ághios* or *áyios*. (By the way, the letter *g* should be pronounced as *y* in *yet* when followed by *e* or *i*.)

In this guide, Greek words are written as they're pronounced today. The traditional anglicized spelling is used for a few widely accepted proper nouns, e.g. Rhodes and proper nouns in a historical context.

Stress, a very important feature of the Greek language, is indicated in our transcription by an acute accent (′) above the vowel of the syllable which should be pronounced louder.

A

You'll find most people in Rhodes Town speak some English, French, German or Italian. Signs are written in both Greek and Latin alphabets. Menus are sometimes available in five languages, including Swedish.

The Greeks themselves have more of a problem: there are, in effect, two Greek languages. *Katharévousa,* an attempt to revive classical Greek in the 19th century after the declaration of independence from the Turks, is hardly spoken today. Nevertheless, it's the official language of the courts, parliament and the cabinet. The mass media use a modified version of *katharévousa.*

The spoken language—and the language of poetry—is called *dimotikí.* It's now being used in school textbooks and is what you'll generally hear. Although the Rhodians have a few expressions of their own, their language is not very different from the Greek heard on the mainland.

Α	**α**	a	as in b**a**r	**Ξ**	**ξ**	x	like **ks** in than**ks**
Β	**β**	v		**Ο**	**ο**	o	as in b**o**ne
Γ	**γ**	g	as in **g**o*	**Π**	**π**	p	
Δ	**δ**	d	like **th** in **th**is	**Ρ**	**ρ**	r	
Ε	**ε**	e	as in g**e**t	**Σ**	**σ, ς**	s	as in ki**ss**
Ζ	**ζ**	z		**Τ**	**τ**	t	
Η	**η**	i	like **ee** in m**ee**t	**Υ**	**υ**	i	like **ee** in m**ee**t
Θ	**θ**	th	as in **th**in	**Φ**	**φ**	f	
Ι	**ι**	i	like **ee** in m**ee**t	**Χ**	**χ**	ch	as in Scottish lo**ch**
Κ	**κ**	k		**Ψ**	**ψ**	ps	as in ti**ps**y
Λ	**λ**	l		**Ω**	**ω**	o	as in b**o**ne
Μ	**μ**	m		**ΟΥ**	**ου**	ou	as in s**ou**p
Ν	**ν**	n					

* except before **i**- and **e**-sounds, when it's pronounced like **y** in **y**es

Good morning	**kaliméra**
Good afternoon	**kalispéra**
Good night	**kaliníkta**
Thank you/You're welcome	**efcharistó/típota**
Please/Goodbye	**parakaló/chérete**

The Berlitz phrase book, Greek for Travellers, covers all situations you're likely to encounter in your travels in Greece.

Does anybody speak English? **Milá kanís angliká?**

A **ANTIQUITIES.** Antiquities may be exported only with the approval of the Archaeological Service and the Greek Ministry of Culture and Science. Lawbreakers face a stiff fine and a prison sentence of up to five years. So if you stumble upon an ancient amphora or buy a "genuine Byzantine icon", make sure you have the appropriate licence for export before you take it home. Check with the Archaeological Service:

Odós Ippotón, tel. 27674, open 7.30 a.m. to 2.30 p.m.

B **BABYSITTERS** *"baby-sitter").* Most restaurants welcome children, but if you prefer to go out alone ask at your hotel desk or your tour or travel agent.

Can you get us a babysitter for tonight?	**Boríte na mas vríte mía "baby-sitter" gi'apópse?**

BICYCLE and MOTORSCOOTER RENTAL* *(enikiásis podiláton/motopodiláton).* In Rhodes Town, rental agencies may be found near Makaríou in the city centre near Platía Evréon Martíron in the Old Town.

In Rhodes Town, no noise from two-wheeled vehicles is permitted during the siesta, after 11 p.m. or in front of hotels.

What's the rental charge for a full day?	**Póso kostízi giá mía iméra?**

BOATS and FERRIES. Whether you take a ferry to Rhodes from the mainland or just a boat trip down the island's east coast, you'll find that travelling by sea is the best way to see the Aegean.

Sailings from Piraeus to Rhodes, a trip of 18 to 20 hours, can be checked with the Tourist Office in Athens; departures from Rhodes are best discovered on the spot. A boat timetable can be obtained from the National or Municipal Tourist Office on Rhodes or phone the port police, tel. 22 220, 28 888 or 27 695.

BUSES* *(leoforío).* The island has generally reliable, well-organized bus services. Fares are relatively low, but at rush hours the buses are very crowded and, in summer, uncomfortably hot. The most hectic scrambling for seats occurs between 1.30 and 2 p.m.

Most buses are boarded at the rear, where conductors issue tickets. Don't forget to hold on to your ticket until the end of the trip; an inspector might come aboard to check. In Rhodes Town catch the bus either at the R.O.D.A. bus station behind Néa Agorá (New Market) along Papagou, or close by at the K.T.E.L. station. Timetables are displayed in the window of the Tourist Information office, and copies are available inside. **B**

When's the next bus to...?	**Póte févgi to epómeno leoforío giá...?**
single (one-way)	**apló**
return (round-trip)	**me epistrofí**

C

CAMPING *("camping").* There are two official campsites on Rhodes: one at Faliráki and a "deluxe" site on the coast at Lárdos, near Líndos, with sports facilities and two swimming pools. Tents may not be pitched anywhere else on the island.

May we camp here?	**Boroúme na kataskinósoume edó?**
We've a tent.	**Échoume mía skiní.**

CAR RENTAL* *(enikiásis aftokiníton).* See also DRIVING IN GREECE. There are dozens of car hire firms in town. But it's wise to book at least a day in advance in high season. Most agencies accept internationally recognized credit cards. Third-party insurance is included in the price but damage to tyres, wheels and the underside of the car is at the renters expense.

Though the International Driving Permit is legally obligatory for all foreigners *hiring* a car in Greece, firms in practice accept virtually any national licence, stipulating that it must have been held for at least one year.

I'd like to rent a car tomorrow.	**Tha íthela na nikiáso éna aftokínito ávrio.**
for one day/a week	**giá mía iméra/mía evdomáda**
Please include full insurance.	**Sas parakaló na simberilávete miktí asfália.**

CIGARETTES, CIGARS, TOBACCO* *(tsigára; poúra; kapnós).* Greek tobacco is world famous. Though most of it comes from Macedonia, there's also tobacco grown on Rhodes. Some of the better known brands of cigarettes are *Astor, Assos Filtro, Karelia, Sertika, Byron, Old Navy* and menthol-flavoured *Mistral.*

A packet of cigarettes/matches.	**Éna pakéto tsigára/spírta.**
filter-tipped/without filter	**me fíltro/chorís fíltro**

C

CLOTHING *(rouchismós)*. Rhodes is informal all year round; generally shorts, slacks and summer skirts and blouses are all that's required. Bear in mind, however, that to visit churches and monasteries, women are expected to be decently covered—no revealing necklines or shorts. In the evening, ties for men are optional; jackets are common at the smarter hotels.

Dress and pack lightly; drip-dry items are most practical. Cotton is preferable to synthetic fabrics in the hot weather. There's often a breeze, so a scarf and a light jacket will prove useful. And if you travel by boat, especially in winter, bring an anorak (parka) or sweater.The *meltémi*, the Aegean north wind, can be nippy.

Don't forget comfortable shoes for visiting difficult sites or hiking. Sandals or rope-soled shoes are useful, and you can buy them cheaply in Rhodes. You may want rubber bathing slippers for stony beaches or shell-encrusted reef.

Women								
Clothing			Shirts / Pullovers			Shoes		
GB	USA	Greece	GB	USA	Greece	GB	USA	Greece
10	8	40	32	10	42	3	4½	35
12	10	42	34	12	44	4	5½	36
14	12	44	36	14	46	5	6½	37
16	14	46	38	16	48	6	7½	38
18	16	48	40	18	50	7	8½	39

Men						
Clothing		Shirts		Shoes		
GB / USA	Greece	GB / USA	Greece	GB	USA	Greece
36	46	14	36	6	6½	39
38	48	14½	37	7	7½	40
40	50	15	38	8	8½	41
42	52	15½	39	9	9½	42
44	54	16	40	10	10½	43

COMMUNICATIONS. The main post and telegraph office, which faces Mandráki, is open Monday to Saturday 7.30 a.m. to 8 p.m. You can also buy stamps from machines or at tobacconists' or wherever postcards are on sale. All outgoing mail goes by air. Note that Greek post-boxes are painted yellow.

C

Mail. There's a poste restante (general delivery) service at the main post office *(tachidromío),* if you don't have a hotel address. Take your passport to the post office for identification.

Telephone *(tiléfono).* The Greek telephone system is linked to most European countries, the U.S.A. and Canada.

The main telephone centre of the Greek Telecommunications Organization (OTE), open from 6 a.m. to midnight, is at the corner of Amerikís and 25is Martíou. OTE also has a sub-office, well signposted, in the Old Town just beyond Platía Argirokástrou (open 7.30 a.m.–3 p.m.).

Telephoning from a booth costs very little for a local call. Blue telephone call-boxes are only for domestic calls. Orange call-boxes, with instructions in English are linked to the international dialling system.

Can you get me this number in...?	**Boríte na mou párete aftó ton arithmó...?**
reverse the charges	**plirotéo apó to paralípti**
personal (person-to-person) call	**prosopikí klísi**
A stamp for this letter/postcard, please.	**Éna grammatósimo giaftó to grámma/kart postál, parakaló.**
I want to send a telegram to...	**Thélo na stílo éna tilegráfima sto...**
Have you received any mail for...?	**Échete grámmata giá...?**

COMPLAINTS *(parápona).* If you really feel you've been cheated or misled, take it up with the manager or owner of the establishment first. Although consumer protection is in its infancy in this country, Greeks are firm believers in fair play in commercial matters.

Still annoyed and unsatisfied? Take your problem to the tourist police (see POLICE, page 119) whose job is to help you. Tourism is a major money-earner for the Greek government, and they want you to go home happy.

C

CONSULATES *(proxenío)*

British Consulate*: Amerikis III (1st floor), Rhodes Town; tel. 272-47, 27306.

Canadian Consulate: Gennadíou 4/Ipsilántou, 115-21 Athens; tel. (01) 7239-511.

U.S. Consulate: Leofóros Vas. Sofías 91, 101-60 Athens; tel. (01) 7212-951.

Many Western European countries have consular offices in Rhodes. All the embassies are in Athens.

If you run into trouble with the authorities or the police, get in touch with your consulate for advice.

Where's the British/American/ Canadian Consulate?	**Pou íne to anglikó/amerikanikó/ kanadikó proxenío?**
It's very urgent.	**Íne polí epígon.**

CONVERTER CHARTS. For tire pressure, distance and fluid measures see pages 111–112. Greece uses the metric system.

Temperature

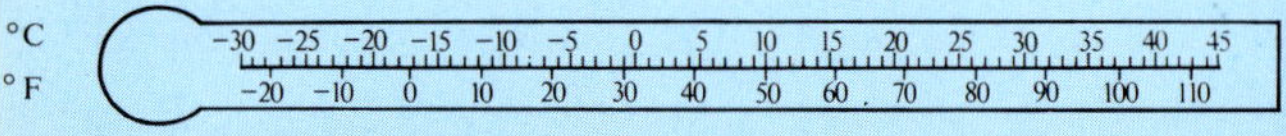

Length

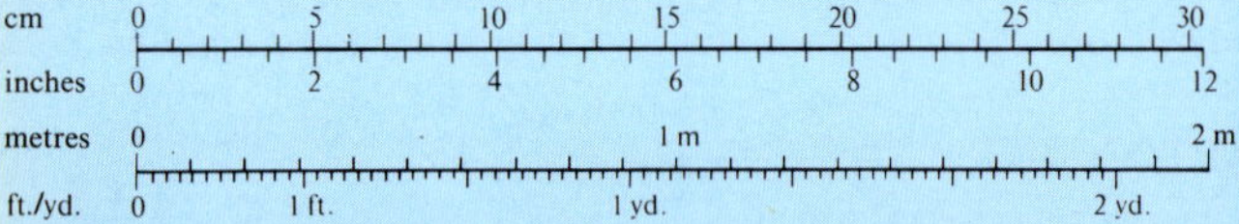

Weight

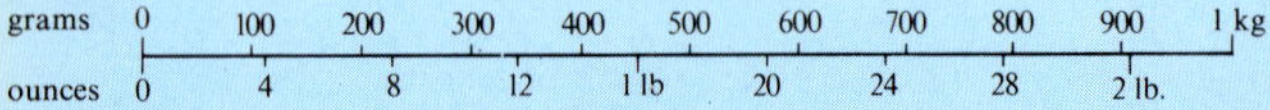

COURTESIES. You'll discover that Greek hospitality is sincere, generous and sometimes overwhelming. Whatever you do, don't turn your back on it.

If a taxi driver offers you a cigarette it's polite to accept. (If you're a non-smoker, just let him know.) He's not looking for a tip. It's his way of

* Also for citizens of Commonwealth countries.

extending you a welcome. Don't turn down an offer of coffee and the inevitable glass of water unless it's obvious somebody is trying hard to sell you something.

It's best not to visit or telephone anyone between 2.30 and 5 p.m. The Greeks take their siestas seriously.

You must avoid waving your hand to someone with the palm facing outwards. Greeks call this gesture *moúntza*—and it's full of ancient evil connotations. So be careful when you wave good-bye or count to five on your fingers.

Staring isn't considered rude in Greece. On the contrary, it's a way of making a compliment or satisfying curiosity (a common Greek trait), and it isn't a sign of bad manners.

Greeks celebrate name days (according to the Orthodox Church calendar) rather than birthdays. You might want to check the names of any local friends against the list for day and month. You should wish them *chrónia pollá* ("many years").

And remember, it's always a good idea to learn a few basic expressions, such as good morning *(kaliméra)*, please *(parakaló)*, thank you *(efcharistó)* and you're welcome *(típota)*. These are niceties guaranteed to win friends. See also ALPHABET AND LANGUAGE.

How are you?	**Ti kánete?**

CRIME and THEFT *(églima; klopí)*. Practically non-existent. In fact, Rhodes has no jail and must send law-breakers (usually traffic violators) to the island of Kos to be locked up. Although hotels request that valuables be put in the safe, there are virtually no instances of items taken from the rooms.

I want to report a theft.	**Thélo na katangílo mía klopí.**

CUSTOMS CONTROLS and ENTRY FORMALITIES. In addition to personal clothing, you can bring in a camera and a reasonable amount of film, binoculars, typewriter, radio, tape recorder, musical instruments and sports equipment. In principle these must be declared when you enter Greece, but you probably won't even be asked. No duty will be charged unless you have more than one of any item per person.

Visitors from EEC (Common Market) countries only need an identity card to enter Greece, but a passport is highly recommended. Citizens of most other countries must be in possession of a valid passport.

The following chart shows the quantities of certain items you may take into Greece and, upon your return home, into your own country:

C

Into:	Cigarettes	Cigars	Tobacco	Spirits	Wine
Greece 1)	300 or	75 or	400 g.	1½ l. and	5 l.
2)	200 or	50 or	250 g.	1 l. or	2 l.
3)	400 or	100 or	500 g.	see 1) and	2)
Canada	200 and	50 and	900 g.	1.1 l. or	1.1 l.
Eire	200 or	50 or	250 g.	1 l. and	2 l.
U.K.	200 or	50 or	250 g.	1 l. and	2 l.
U.S.A.	200 and	100 or	4)	1 l. or	1 l.

1) Residents of Europe, non-duty-free items purchased in EEC countries (alcoholic beverage allowances—also for non-European residents)
2) Residents of Europe, items purchased outside EEC countries or in EEC countries duty-free (alcoholic beverage allowances—also for non-European residents)
3) Residents outside Europe
4) A reasonable quantity

Certain prescription drugs, including tranquilizers and headache preparations, cannot be carried into the country without a prescription or official document. Fines or even jail sentences have been imposed on the unwary tourist.

Currency restrictions: Non-residents may import up to 25,000 drachmas and export up to 10,000 drachmas (in denominations no larger than 1,000 drachmas). There's no limit on the foreign currency or traveller's cheques you may import or export, though amounts in excess of $1,000 or its equivalent must be declared to the customs official upon arrival.

I've nothing to declare. **Den écho na dilóso típota.**

D

DRIVING IN GREECE. To bring your car into Greece you'll need:

International Driving Permit (see below)	car registration papers	Insurance coverage (the Green Card is no longer obligatory within the EEC but comprehensive coverage is advisable).
	nationality plate or sticker	

The Green Card is not required of citizens of EEC countries, but it's still preferable to have it. The International Driving Permit (not required for British motorists) can be obtained through your home motoring association.

If you have a breakdown, get in touch with the car-rental agency which rented you the car. See also EMERGENCIES section.

The standard European red warning triangle is required for emergencies. Wearing seat-belts is now obligatory in Greece. Motorcycle and motorscooter drivers—as well as passengers—must wear crash helmets.

Driving conditions on Rhodes: The highways on Rhodes are good around Rhodes Town, but they get progressively worse—with a profusion of potholes—as you head south on the island. Careful driving is required on narrow and winding roads. Watch out particularly for approaching tourist buses—and goats, cows or oxen straying into your path. Don't be afraid to use your horn when rounding blind corners. Greeks blast away and expect the same from oncoming traffic.

From March to October cars are not allowed into Rhodes Old Town between 6 a.m. and 10 a.m. Parking is very restricted at all times.

Trafic Police: see POLICE

Fuel and oil: Service stations are now plentiful on the island, but check your tank before heading for the more remote areas in the south. Opening hours are 7 a.m. to 7 p.m. One station in a radius of 14 km stays open till midnight. You can find their details posted in other stations in the area.

Distances

From Rhodes Town:

Archángelos 32 km; Lindos 54.5 km; Petaloúdes 24 km.

To convert kilometres into miles:

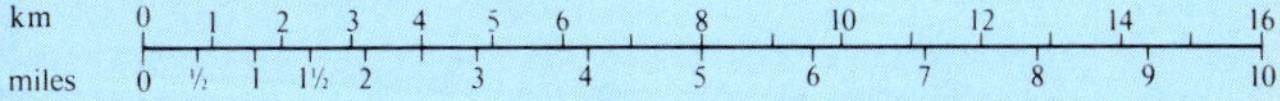

Fluid measures

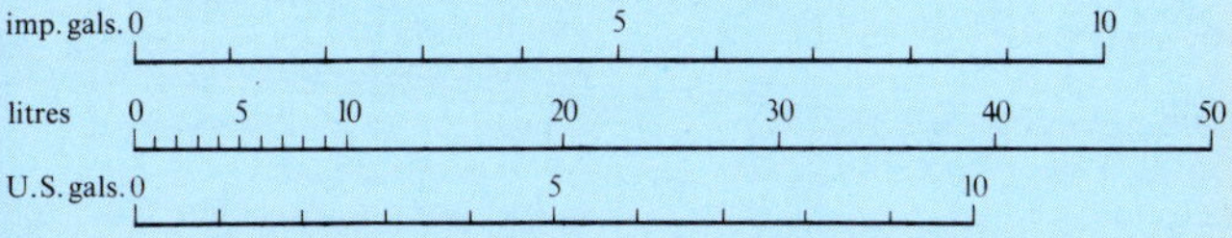

D

Tire pressure

lb./sq. in.	kg/cm²	lb./sq. in.	kg/cm²
10	0.7	26	1.8
12	0.8	27	1.9
15	1.1	28	2.0
18	1.3	30	2.1
20	1.4	33	2.3
21	1.5	36	2.5
23	1.6	38	2.7
24	1.7	40	2.8

Road signs: Most road signs are the standard pictographs used throughout Europe. However, you may encounter the following written signs on Rhodes:

ΑΔΙΕΞΟΔΟΣ	No through road
ΑΛΤ	Stop
ΑΝΩΜΑΛΙΑ ΟΔΟΣΤΡΩΜΑΤΟΣ	Bad road surface
ΑΠΑΓΟΡΕΥΕΤΑΙ Η ΑΝΑΜΟΝΗ	No waiting
ΑΠΑΓΟΡΕΥΕΤΑΙ Η ΕΙΣΟΔΟΣ	No entry
ΑΠΑΓΟΡΕΥΕΤΑΙ Η ΣΤΑΘΜΕΥΣΙΣ	No parking
ΔΙΑΒΑΣΙΣ ΠΕΖΩΝ	Pedestrian crossing
ΕΛΑΤΤΩΣΑΤΕ ΤΑΧΥΤΗΤΑΝ	Reduce speed
ΕΠΙΚΙΝΔΥΝΟΣ ΚΑΤΩΦΕΡΕΙΑ	Dangerous incline
ΕΡΓΑ ΕΠΙ ΤΗΣ ΟΔΟΥ	Roadworks in progress (Men working)
ΚΙΝΔΥΝΟΣ	Caution
ΜΟΝΟΔΡΟΜΟΣ	One-way traffic
ΠΑΡΑΚΑΜΠΤΗΡΙΟΣ	Diversion (Detour)
ΠΟΔΗΛΑΤΑΙ	Cyclists
ΠΟΡΕΙΑ ΥΠΟΧΡΕΩΤΙΚΗ ΔΕΞΙΑ	Keep right
ΣΤΑΣΙΣ ΛΕΩΦΟΡΕΙΟΥ	Bus stop

(International) Driving Licence	**(diethnís) ádia odigíseos**
car registration papers	**ádia kikloforías**
Green Card	**asfália aftokinítou**
Are we on the right road for ...?	**Ímaste sto sostó drómo giá ...?**
Fill her up, please, top grade.	**Na to gemísete me venzíni soúper, parakaló.**

Check the oil/tyres/battery.	**Na elénxete ta ládia/ta lásticha/ ti bataría.**
I've had a breakdown.	**Épatha mía vlávi.**
There's been an accident.	**Égine éna distíchima.**

D

DRUGS. Smuggling hard and soft drugs into the country carries severe penalties—up to seven years imprisonment.

E

EARTHQUAKES. Don't let it shake you up, but you should know that Rhodes is on a fault line and has quite a history, geologically speaking. Earthquakes seem to average about two a century. The 20th century has already fulfilled its quake quota—1926 and 1957.

ELECTRIC CURRENT *(ilektrikó révma).* You will find only 220-volt, 50-cycle A.C.

an adaptor	**énas metaschimatistís**
a battery	**mía bataría**

EMERGENCIES *(prótes anánges).* If your hotel receptionist isn't around to help, here are a few essential telephone numbers:

Police	100	Tourist police	233-29/274-23
Fire	199	Traffic police	223-46
First Aid	222-22	Motorists' Road Assistance (ELPA)	104
Tourist office	232-55		

Depending on the nature of the emergency, refer to the separate entries in this section such as CONSULATES, HEALTH, POLICE, etc.

Though we hope you'll never need them, here are a few words you might like to learn in advance:

Careful	**Prosochí**
Fire	**Fotiá**
Help	**Voïthia**
Stop	**Stamatíste**

G

GUIDES and INTERPRETERS *(xenagós; dierminéas).* The official guide service of the Dodecanese has a highly skilled staff of about 70. They have guides in English and European languages.

Their address: Karpáthou, tel. 275-25.

G If you're interested in knowledgeable guidance at sites, the tourist-information office can refer you to an officially recognized guide.

We'd like an English-speaking guide.	**Tha thélame éna xenagó na milá i angliká.**
I need an English interpreter.	**Chriázome éna ánglo dierminéa.**

H **HAIRDRESSERS'*** *(kommotírio)*. You'll find women's and men's hairdressers' in the centre of town or in large hotels. Following are some phrases which you might find useful:

haircut	**koúrema**
shampoo and set	**loúsimo ke miz-an-plí**
blow-dry	**chténisma me to pistoláki**
permanent wave	**permanád**
a colour chart	**éna digmatológio**
a colour rinse	**mía dekolorasión**
Not too much off (here).	**Óchi polí kondá (edó).**
A little more off (here).	**Lígo pió kondá (edó).**

HEALTH and MEDICAL CARE. To avoid severe sunburn, which ruins many holidays, bask for only short periods for the first few days, and even with a "base tan", beware of the Aegean sun between 11 a.m. and 2 p.m. Moderation in eating and drinking should spare you most stomach upsets travellers experience with a change of diet. Mosquitos are a problem on various islands. You'll find on sale an inflammable coil device called *Katól,* which keeps them out of your bedroom. There are also repellent lotions.

Should you be stung by a medusa (jellyfish), apply ammonia immediately to relieve the pain. If there's severe swelling or any other complication, unfailingly see a doctor.

Do your eyes a favour and wear sunglasses. You may never have seen the sun so brightly and glaringly reflected.

To be completely relaxed, make certain your health-insurance policy covers any illness or accident while on holiday. If not, ask your insurance representative about travel insurance. Tourists can also obtain coverage from Greek insurance companies.

There are many competent doctors and dentists on the island. Perhaps it's because Hippocrates, father of modern medicine, was born and raised on the nearby island of Kos. Your hotel should be able to suggest a bilingual doctor or dentist. A hospital in Rhodes Town is open 24 hours to deal with emergencies, tel. 222-22. See also EMERGENCIES.

Chemists' shops, or drugstores *(farmakíon).* You can recognize a *farmakíon* by the sign hanging outside—a red (or sometimes blue) cross on a white background. There is always one pharmacy in town open all night and on Sundays for emergencies. Pharmacies are allowed to sell antibiotics without prescription and they are a good source of advice regarding minor medical problems.

a doctor/a dentist	**énas giatrós/énas odontogiatrós**
an ambulance	**éna asthenofóro**
hospital	**nosokomío**
an upset stomach	**varistomachiá**
sunstroke	**ilíasi**
a fever	**piretós**

HITCH-HIKING *(oto-stóp).* It's legal everywhere in Greece, and you shouldn't run into too many difficulties obtaining a ride.

Can you give us a lift to...?	**Boríte na mas páte méchri to...?**

HOTELS and ACCOMMODATION* *(xenodochío; domátia).* Hotels are in categories running from luxury to modest establishments. Rooms in private homes are often available in outlying areas. Altogether, about 30,000 beds are available and the number grows each year. Nearly all the hotels are in Rhodes Town or grouped along the western coast. Book in advance, for Rhodes is the most sought-after holiday island of Greece, particularly in July and August. If you do happen to arrive without a room, inquire at the City of Rodos Tourist Information Office desk at the airport.

Unless you're on an all-inclusive package tour, you'll normally receive a weekly bill. Price reductions can usually be arranged for children. In full season, the hotel management may insist on your taking half or full board. If your room has no private bath or shower, you may be charged a little extra for hot water in the bathroom down the hall. All service charges are included in the rates, which must be posted in your room. They're also listed in a comprehensive index at

H the National Tourist Organization of Greece and most travel agents. When air-conditioning is provided, a slight extra charge is added to the bill.

Rooms must be left usually by noon on the day of departure. You're subject to extra charges after that hour.

a double/single room with/without bath	**éna dipló/monó domátio me/chorís bánio**
What's the rate per night?	**Piá íne i timí giá mía níkta?**

HOURS. Napping or resting during the heat of the day is a sensible, old Mediterranean habit. The Greek lunch period blends into siesta time, and cash registers stop ringing between 1.30 and 5 p.m. Note that noise—especially from motorbikes—is not at all appreciated during this period. Work resumes at 5 until perhaps 9 p.m.

Banks and Currency-Exchange Offices: 8 a.m. to 2 p.m. Monday to Friday. National Bank, Cyprus Square reopens 3.30 to 8 or 8.30 p.m., and Saturday and Sunday 9 a.m.–noon for currency exchange.

Pharmacies: 8 a.m. to 1 p.m., 5 p.m. to 9 p.m. Monday to Friday; Saturday 8 a.m. to 2 p.m. Outside these hours, notices posted in pharmacy windows indicate the nearest one on duty.

Post Office: 7.30 a.m. to 8.30 p.m., Monday to Friday.

Tourist Office (at Platía Rímini): 8 a.m. to 7.30 p.m.

L **LAUNDRY and DRY CLEANING** (ΠΛΥΝΤΗΡΙΟ—*plintírio;* ΚΑΘΑΡΙΣΤΗΡΙΟ—*katharistírio*). Washing and dry cleaning is expensive whether done by your hotel or at a local establishment. There are a couple of dry cleaners in the New Town, and there is also a coin-operated launderette on 28. octovrion.

When will it be ready?	**Póte tha íne étimo?**
I must have this for tomorrow morning.	**Prépi na íne étimo ávrio te proï.**

LOST PROPERTY *(grafio apolesthéndon andikiménon)*; **LOST CHILDREN.** If you really think your child has vanished, call the tourist police (telephone 274-23). They'll probably discover him at a local café being fed and entertained by friendly Greeks.

As for property dont' worry too much. If you've lost or mislaid something you have a very good chance of getting it back. Call the Lost and Found Office, tel. 232-94.

I've lost my wallet/handbag/ passport.	**Échasa to portofóli mou/ti tsánda mou/to diavatirió mou.**

L

MAPS *(chártis)*. There are several maps of the region for sale on the island.

a street plan of...	**éna odikó chárti tou...**
a road map of the island	**éna chárti tou nisioú**

M

MONEY MATTERS. The monetary unit of Greece is the drachma (*drachmí,* abbreviated Δρχ.).

There are coins of 1, 2, 5, 10, 20, 50 and 100 drachmas.

Banknotes come in denominations of 100, 500, 1,000 and 5,000 drachmas.

Banks and Currency-Exchange Offices *(trápeza; sinállagma)*. There are branch offices of leading Greek banks on the island. They are open Monday to Friday; Saturdays, Sundays and holidays some banks may be open in the morning but only for currency-exchange transactions. Most are grouped near Makaríou and Platía Kíprou in the heart of the shopping district. You'll normally receive a better exchange rate in the banks than at your hotel. In addition, traveller's cheques and Eurocheques will get a slightly better rate than cash.

Always take your passport with you when you go to exchange money.

Credit Cards and Traveller's Cheques *(pistotikí kárta; "traveller's cheque")*. Internationally known credit cards are honoured in most shops and by all banks, car-hire firms and leading hotels in Rhodes. But when dining out in local *tavérnes* or dancing away the evening in a discotheque, take Greek currency along to be sure.

Major brands of traveller's cheques are easily cashed, but take your passport with you for identification.

I want to change some pounds/ dollars.	**Thélo na alláxo merikés líres/ dollária.**

M Do you accept traveller's cheques? — **Pérnete "traveller's cheques"?**

Can I pay with this credit card? — **Boró na pliróso me aftí ti pistotikí kárta?**

N **NEWSPAPERS and MAGAZINES** *(efimerída; periodikó).* Most foreign dailies—including the principal British newspapers and the Paris-based *International Herald Tribune*—arrive on Rhodes one day late. For faster news in English, you can pick up the *Athens News.* The free English-language newspaper *Rhodes Gazette,* published from April to end-October, is available at the tourist office.

Most hotels have news-stands. For the biggest selection of foreign newspapers and magazines, go to the news-stand in the arcaded entry to the market-place at Mandráki harbour or to the bookstalls just in front of the post office.

Have you any English-language newspapers? — **Échete anglikés efimerídes?**

P **PETS and VETS** *(zóa; ktiníatros).* If you plan to bring your dog, you'll need a veterinary health certificate stating that the animal has been vaccinated against rabies within the past 12 months. Cats need a certificate guaranteeing that they're free of contagious disease.

Either certificate is supposed to be stamped by your nearest Greek consulate to facilitate entry. Confirm this before your departure.

Keep in mind that hotels generally do not allow pets.

Returning to Great Britain or Eire, your pet will have to go through six months of quarantine for having spent time in a country that is not rabies free. Both the U.S. and Canada reserve the right to impose quarantine.

PHOTOGRAPHY. A photo shop is advertised by the sign ΦΩΤΟΓΡΑΦΕΙΟ *(fotografío).* Major brands of colour and black-and-white film for still and cinecameras are widely available on Rhodes, but prices are no bargains—it's probably best to buy film before your holiday and take it home for processing.

Hand-held photo equipment may be used in all museums and on archaeological sites, but you must pay a nominal fee for their use.

 Tripods are subject to heavy entry fees since they're considered the mark of a professional, not of an amateur photographer. So you may prefer to deposit yours at the entrance.

For security reasons, it's illegal to use a telephoto lens aboard an aircraft flying over Greece. But there are no restrictions on ordinary still and cinecameras.

I'd like a film for this camera.	**Tha íthela éna film giaftí ti michaní.**
black-and-white film	**asprómavro film**
colour prints	**énchromo film**
35-mm film	**éna film triánda pénde milimétr**
colour slides	**énchromo film giá sláïds**
super-8	**soúper-októ**
How long will it take to develop (and print) this film?	**Se póses iméres boríte na emfanísete (ke na ektipósete) aftó to film?**

POLICE *(astinomía)*. There are two kinds of police on Rhodes. Regular police (called *chorofilakes)* wear green uniforms. They are particularly severe on speeding violations and can fine you on the spot.

The *Touristikí Astinomía* (tourist police) are a branch of the police force. The distinctive patches (national flags) sewn on their dark grey uniforms indicate foreign languages spoken. The tourist police have the authority to inspect prices in restaurants and hotels. If you've a complaint, these are the people to see.

Where's the nearest police station?	**Pou íne to kodinótero astinomikó tmíma?**

PUBLIC HOLIDAYS *(argíes)*. Banks, offices and shops are closed on the following national holidays:

Movable dates:	*Katharí Deftéra*	1st Day of Lent: Clean Monday
	Megáli Paraskeví	Good Friday
	Deftéra tou Páscha	Easter Monday
	Análipsis	Ascension
	tou Agíou Pnévmatos	Whit Monday ("Holy Spirit")

P

Jan. 1	*Protochroniá*	New Year's Day
Jan. 6	*ton Theofanion*	Epiphany
March 25	*Ikostí Pémti Martíou (tou Evangelismoú)*	Greek Independence Day
May 1	*Protomagiá*	May Day
Aug. 15	*Dekapendávgoustos (tis Panagías)*	Assumption Day
Oct. 28	*Ikostí Ogdóï Oktovríou*	*Óchi* ("no") Day, commemorating Greek defiance of Italian ultimatum and invasion of 1940
Dec. 25	*Christoúgenna*	Christmas Day
Dec. 26	*défteri iméra ton Christougénnon*	St. Stephen's Day

Note: The dates on which the movable holy days are celebrated often differ from those in Catholic and Protestant countries.

Are you open tomorrow? **Échete aniktá ávrio?**

R

RADIO and TV *(rádio; tileórasi).* Greek National Radio broadcasts news in English from Monday to Friday around 6 p.m. in season. The Voice of America operates a relay transmitter on Rhodes, just outside the village of Koskinoú. While most broadcasting is in Arabic and Turkish, a world-news summary in English is broadcast in the morning and at midnight. The tourist office or your hotel desk can provide you with a broadcast schedule. Some hotels have television lounges.

RELIGIOUS SERVICES *(litourgía).* The national church of Greece is Greek Orthodox.

There's no Anglican or other Protestant congregation on Rhodes. However, inquire at St. Mary's Catholic church on Kathopoúli, Rhodes Town, since visiting clergymen sometimes conduct Protestant services there during the tourist season. At St. Mary's church, mass is said in Latin, on weekdays at 7 p.m. and on Sundays at 8 and 11 a.m. and 7 p.m. In season, part of the mass may be in English.

What time is mass/the service?	**Ti óra archízi i litourgía?**
Is it in English?	**Íne sta angliká?**

RESTAURANTS* *(estiatórion; tavérna).* Getting something to eat or drink is usually no problem at all for a visitor to Rhodes. Many places have menus in foreign languages or, better yet, just follow the local practice of sauntering into the kitchen, looking over the day's dishes and pointing to your choice. But, you may find the following terms useful.

Could we have a table?	**Tha boroúsame na échoume éna trapézi?**
I'd like a/an/some...	**Tha íthela...**

beer	**mía bíra**	mineral water	**metallikó neró**
bread	**psomí**	napkin	**éna trapezo-mándilo**
coffee	**éna kafé**	potatoes	**patátes**
cutlery	**machero-pírouna**	rice	**rízi**
dessert	**éna glikó**	salad	**mía saláta**
fish	**psári**	sandwich	**éna sánduïts**
fruit	**froúta**	soup	**mía soúpa**
glass	**éna potíri**	sugar	**záchari**
ice-cream	**éna pagotó**	tea	**éna tsáï**
meat	**kréas**	(iced) water	**(pagoméno) neró**
milk	**gála**	wine	**krasí**

TAXIS *(taxí).* Despite high fuel prices, taxis continue to be inexpensive on Rhodes—and drivers are helpful and honest. The city version has TAΞI written on the roof. Another type of taxi is the *agoréon*. It's the rural vehicle, found only outside city limits. There is no meter, but rates are fixed for specific distances or zones. (It works out slightly higher than meter prices.) Hiring a taxi for the day or for several hours is subject to negotiation. To order a taxi *amésos* (quickly), telephone 27666. That's the main taxi rank just off Mandráki harbour. Tip about 10 per cent, although drivers actually expect only a rounding off of the fare.

What's the fare to...?	**Piá íne i timí giá...?**

T

TIME DIFFERENCES. Since Greece goes on summer time at about the same time as the British Isles, there's a two-hour difference between the countries all year round. During the holiday season, there are variations because of the summer-time schedules, but here's the normal time difference in summer:

Los Angeles	Chicago	New York	London	**Rhodes**
2 a.m.	4 a.m.	5 a.m.	10 a.m.	**noon**

What time is it? **Ti óra íne?**

TIPPING. By law, service charges are included in the bill at hotels, restaurants and *tavérnes*. The Greeks aren't tip-crazy, but they do expect you to leave a little more—if the service has been good, of course.

Even if your room or meals are included as part of a package tour, you'll still want to remember the maid and the waiter. The waiter will probably have a *mikró* (an assistant, or busboy), who should get a token of appreciation as well.

Hotel porter, ber bag	30–50 drs.
Maid, per day	100 drs.
Waiter	5% (optional)
Lavatory attendant	20 drs.
Taxi driver	10% (optional)
Tour guide	100–200 drs. (optional)
Hairdresser/Barber	10%

TOILETS. Nowadays, Rhodes Town is well enough supplied with public toilets at crucial points. You can, of course, also try a café or *tavérna*. Sign language or a ΤΟΥΑΛΕΤΤΕΣ sign ought to direct you to a couple of doors marked ΑΝΔΡΩΝ (gentlemen) and ΓΥΝΑΙΚΩΝ (ladies).

Where are the toilets? **Pou íne i toualéttes?**

TOURIST INFORMATION OFFICES *(grafío pliroforión tourismoú).* The central headquarters of the Greek National Tourist Organization (*Ellinikós Organismós Tourismoú,* abbreviated EOT) is in Athens at Amerikís 2 (tel. 3223-111/9). T

Outside the country, the offices below will supply you with a wide range of colourful and informative brochures and maps in English. They'll also let you consult the master directory of hotels in Greece, listing all facilities and prices.

British Isles: 4 Conduit Street London W1R ODJ; tel: (071) 734-5997

U.S.A.: 645 5th Ave., New York, NY 10022; tel.: (212) 421-5777;
611 W. 6th St., Los Angeles, CA 90017; tel.: (213) 626-6696;
168 N. Michigan Ave., Chicago, IL 60601; tel.: 641-6600, 782-1084;

Canada: 80 Bloor St. West, Suite 1403, Toronto, On. M5S 2VI; tel.: (416) 968-2220;
1233 rue de la Montagne, Montreal, Que. H3G 1Z2; tel.: (514) 871-1535.

In Rhodes Town, the City of Rodos Tourist Information Office in Platía Rímini (see also HOURS) is staffed with an efficient, multilingual personnel. There are branch offices at the harbour and the airport.

Where's the tourist office?	**Pou íne to grafío tourismoú?**

WATER *(neró).* Not only is the island's tap water safe to drink, but village connoisseurs debate the special qualities and taste of waters from particular springs. Greeks usually serve water as a chaser for alcoholic drinks and coffee. Bottled mineral water is also available at bars and restaurants. W

a bottle of mineral water	**éna boukáli metallikó neró**
fizzy (carbonated)	**me anthrakikó**
still	**chorís anthrakikó**
Is this drinking water?	**Íne pósimo aftó to neró?**

DAYS OF THE WEEK

Sunday	**Kiriakí**	Thursday	**Pémti**
Monday	**Deftéra**	Friday	**Paraskeví**
Tuesday	**Tríti**	Saturday	**Sávvato**
Wednesday	**Tetárti**		

MONTHS

January	**Ianouários**	July	**Ioúlios**
February	**Fevrouários**	August	**Ávgoustos**
March	**Mártios**	September	**Septémvrios**
April	**Aprílios**	October	**Októvrios**
May	**Máïos**	November	**Noémvrios**
June	**Ioúnios**	December	**Dekémvrios**

NUMBERS

1	**éna**	19	**dekaenniá**
2	**dío**	20	**íkosi**
3	**tría**	21	**íkosi éna**
4	**téssera**	22	**íkosi dío**
5	**pénde**	30	**triánda**
6	**éxi**	31	**triánda éna**
7	**eptá**	32	**triánda dío**
8	**októ**	40	**saránda**
9	**enniá**	50	**penínda**
10	**déka**	60	**exínda**
11	**éndeka**	70	**evdomínda**
12	**dódeka**	80	**ogdónda**
13	**dekatría**	90	**enenínda**
14	**dekatéssera**	100	**ekató**
15	**dekapénde**	101	**ekatón éna**
16	**dekaéxi**	102	**ekatón dío**
17	**dekaeptá**	500	**pendakósia**
18	**dekaoktó**	1,000	**chília**

SOME USEFUL EXPRESSIONS

yes/no	**ne/óchi**
please/thank you	**parakaló/efcharistó**
excuse me/you're welcome	**me sinchoríte/típota**
where/when/how	**pou/póte/pos**
how long/how far	**póso keró/póso makriá**
yesterday/today/tomorrow	**chthes/símera/ávrio**
day/week/month/year	**iméra/evdomáda/mínas/chrónos**
left/right	**aristerá/dexiá**
up/down	**epáno/káto**
good/bad	**kalós/kakós**
big/small	**megálos/mikrós**
cheap/expensive	**ftinós/akrivós**
hot/cold	**zestós/kríos**
old/new	**paliós/néos**
open/closed	**aniktós/klistós**
Does anyone here speak English?	**Milá kanís angliká?**
I don't understand.	**Den katalavéno.**
Please write it down.	**Parakaló grápste to.**
What does this mean?	**Ti siméni aftó?**
What time is it?	**Ti óra íne?**
How much is that?	**Póso káni aftó?**
I'd like...	**Tha íthela...**
Where are the toilets?	**Pou íne i toualéttes?**
Waiter, please!	**Parakaló!**
Can you help me, please?	**Voïthíste me, parakaló.**
Call a doctor—quickly!	**Kaléste éna giatró—grígora!**
What do you want?	**Ti thélete?**
Just a minute.	**Éna leptó.**
Go away!	**Fígete!**

Index

An asterisk (*) next to a page number indicates a map reference.

INDEX

179/302 MUD.